THE
Persian
Legacy
AND THE
EDGAR CAYCE
MATERIAL

Books by Kevin J. Todeschi

The Edgar Cayce Ideals Workbook
Edgar Cayce on Soul Mates
Edgar Cayce on the Akashic Records
Edgar Cayce on the Reincarnation of Biblical Characters
Edgar Cayce on the Reincarnation of Famous People
Edgar Cayce's ESP
The Encyclopedia of Symbolism
The Persian Legacy and the Edgar Cayce Material
*Soul Development: Edgar Cayce's
Approach for a New World*
Twelve Lessons in Personal Spirituality

THE
Persian
Legacy
AND THE
EDGAR CAYCE
MATERIAL

by Kevin J. Todeschi

ARE
PRESS

ASSOCIATION FOR
RESEARCH AND
ENLIGHTENMENT

A.R.E. Press • Virginia Beach • Virginia

A.R.E. Press
215 67th Street
Virginia Beach, VA 23451-2061

Todeschi, Kevin J.
    The Persian legacy and the Edgar Cayce material / Kevin J.
Todeschi.
        p.   cm.
    Includes bibliographical references.
    ISBN 0-87604-473-9
    1. Cayce, Edgar, 1877-1945. 2. Zoroastrianism. I. Title.
BF1027.C3 T635   2000
133.8092—dc21

                                            00-040128

Cover design by Lightbourne

To My Persian Brothers:
Ahmed and Shigeru

Before that we find the entity was in the land now known as the Persian or Arabian, about that city builded in the "hills and the plains," about that now *known as or called Shushtar in Persia or Arabia.*

991-1

Contents

Introduction

Many people may be aware of the wealth of information contained in Edgar Cayce's psychic "readings" that describe an advanced civilization in ancient Egypt around 10,500 B.C., predating recorded history. Far fewer realize that Cayce also described a subsequent culture in ancient Persia, one rivaling much that Egypt had to offer. Apparently, many of the same souls who had taken Egypt to the height of its glory returned approximately 2,000 years later to give birth to a glorious desert city that served as a center of healing, commerce, and spiritual ministry. Of the more than 14,000 transcribed readings left behind by Cayce, more than 600 discuss ancient Persia, its desert peoples, and a civilization that laid the groundwork for what became the Zoroastrian religion.

The readings' fascination with Persia resulted from the soul history of Edgar Cayce himself. According to

Cayce's own past-life readings, after his experience in ancient Egypt as the high priest, Ra Ta, his next notable incarnation was as Uhjltd (pronounced "Yoo-lt"). This Uhjltd was a Persian nomad who guided a desert people to establish what became the magnificent city of Is-Shlan-doen, frequently referred to as "the city in the hills and the plains," or—according to the readings—also called "Toaz" by the Greeks. During this same lifetime, Cayce's twentieth-century wife, Gertrude, and his secretary, Gladys Davis, had important roles, Gladys as Uhjltd's wife, Ilya, and Gertrude as his niece and adopted daughter, Inxa.

The information on Persia can be traced back to November 7, 1923. On that date, Edgar Cayce gave a reading inquiring about the past-life connections among himself and three people who were interested in financing Cayce's psychic work: Arthur Lammers, a printer from Ohio; Linden Shroyer, an accountant; and George Klingensmith, a construction engineer. During the course of the reading, Cayce mentioned that Lammers had once lived in Arabia in a past life and that it was simply "a thing of fact" (5717-5) that the remains of his body from that lifetime could still be found in a cave seven and one-quarter miles southwest from the present-day Iranian city of Shushtar. No mention of his name in that life was given, and no follow-up questions regarding the activity with which he had been involved were asked at that time.

The lack of follow-up questions was due, in part, to the relative newness of the information on reincarnation to Edgar Cayce. Arthur Lammers had obtained the first reading mentioning the possibility of reincarnation only one month earlier.[1] That reading opened up an entirely

---

[1]Although the first reading to mention reincarnation was in 1923, years later, Gladys Davis discovered that the concept actually was implied in a physical reading given in 1911 (4841-1). No one among Cayce's associates recognized the reference or what it meant for decades, however.

new area of research for Cayce's psychic work, which had previously been focused primarily on health readings and the treatment of illness and disease.

Two weeks later, Gladys Davis, Cayce's secretary and stenographer, requested a life reading for herself (288-1). That reading discussed a series of past lives, including a brief mention of a Persian incarnation when she had studied and been close to the only daughter of Croesus II, ruler of Lydia. Again, no name in that incarnation was given, and no follow-up questions regarding that lifetime were asked.

It was not until February 9, 1924, that Edgar Cayce finally gave his first full-length life reading on himself (294-8). The reading stated that many of the conditions with which Cayce was involved in the present were similar to his incarnation in Persia, when he had been a leader named Uhjltd. The reading alluded to the fact that a near-death experience in that lifetime had further reinforced his psychic abilities and that those abilities remained with him in the present. Within the next year, additional past-life readings for others explored the Uhjltd period in greater detail. Those readings included a past-life reading for Cayce's wife, Gertrude (538-9), as well as a follow-up reading for Gladys, in which she asked about the past-life connection between herself and Edgar Cayce (288-6).

From that time forward, when people received past-life readings, which came to be called "life readings," many learned of their own connection to ancient Persia during the Uhjltd period. What unfolded was a view of reincarnation in which souls tend to incarnate in cyclic patterns, encountering the same souls with whom they have been together previously. Years later, psychologist Gina Cerminara, in her book, *Many Mansions* (1950), a classic exploration of the concepts of reincarnation and karma, noted how certain eras of history were often mentioned repeatedly in the soul histories of Cayce's contemporaries. This process of "group" reincarnation enabled souls to pick up relationships and interactions with one another exactly where they had left off, giving them the opportunity to learn from past mistakes, deal with any unresolved issues, and continue to cultivate positive relationships while attempting to heal negative ones.

One cyclic group sequence of lifetimes that can be seen in the readings includes incarnations in Atlantis, ancient Egypt, ancient Persia, Rome or Palestine at the time of Jesus, the Crusades, eighteenth-century Europe, the American colonial period, and the American Civil War. To be sure, whenever Cayce detailed the soul history of an individual, he always stressed that only those incarnations having a direct bearing on the immediate present were being given. Subsequent readings often detailed additional lifetimes that had not been as relevant at the time of the first reading. From the Cayce files, it becomes clear that those souls have had many more incarnations than those discussed in their past-life readings. The cyclic nature of reincarnation was also noted in May 1948, when Gladys Davis compiled a list of approximately fifty of Cayce's closest contemporaries who also had been associated with one another in both ancient Egypt and ancient Persia (Case 294-153 Reports). However, the actual number of readings that discuss incarnations in both ancient Egypt and ancient Persia totals well over 400.

Although the Uhjltd history and story of Is-Shlandoen, the city in the hills and the plains, were explored in many subsequent readings, it was not until January 1932 that the story of ancient Persia received a major boost. During that month, Jewish businessman Harry M. Goetz, one-time treasurer of Paramount Pictures and president and treasurer of his own, small Reliance Pictures, received his first life reading. Referred by longtime Cayce friend and supporter David Kahn, Goetz had obtained a reading about his business associates only three days earlier. He had been so impressed with the information he received that a follow-up reading detailing his own past lives was immediately scheduled.

During the course of the reading, Cayce informed Goetz that the two of them had once worked together previously. In Is-Shlan-doen, Goetz apparently served Uhjltd as a kind of secretary and minister of state. His name at the time was Edssi, and he gained in soul development for his efforts in carrying Uhjltd's philosophy and teachings to people throughout the land. During the same period, however, Goetz apparently lost at a soul level because of his misuse of mystic information, as well as a tendency to be somewhat pompous in his dealings with others.

In April of that same year, Goetz suggested that the story of Uhjltd and the Persian history actually had the makings of a movie script. A series of readings was given between April and July (294-142 through 294-146) to obtain an outline of the movie scenario, as well as to discuss the draft of a manuscript detailing the story that would be compiled by Edgar Cayce's twenty-five-year-old son, Hugh Lynn. In spite of Goetz's original enthusiasm for the project, the manuscript was found unsuitable, and the movie was never made. It was not until August 1935 that the A.R.E. finally decided to publish Hugh Lynn's fictionalized account of the story as a service to those who wanted to learn more about the Uhjltd period outlined in their own life readings.[2]

Decades passed before the Persian history was further

---

[2]Hugh Lynn Cayce's 1935 publication, simply entitled *Uhjltd*, was an 8,500-word pamphlet that provided a fictionalized account of the story of ancient Persia described in the readings. The entire manuscript has been included in the appendix.

explored in an article written by Lytle Robinson and published in *The A.R.E. Journal* in October 1967. Years earlier, Robinson had received his own Cayce life reading, and he eventually wrote and published two books: *Edgar Cayce's Story of the Origin and Destiny of Man* (1972) and *Is It True What They Say About Edgar Cayce?* (1979). Robinson's article, "The Beginning of Zoroastrianism," concluded with some extracts from the readings that discussed various aspects of the Persian period. For the first time in print, that 1967 article referred to information contained in the readings that Zoroastrianism originated not from Zoroaster but from his father, Zend. What was, perhaps, most notable about the information is that the readings say Zend was an earlier lifetime of the same soul who eventually incarnated as Jesus. Apparently, this Christ soul had long ago chosen to be instrumental in assisting in the development of any religious movement that taught the interconnectedness of humanity and the love and supremacy of the one true God.

The Cayce readings suggest that Zend compiled the Zend-Avesta, the Zoroastrian Bible, and that those teachings were then disseminated by Zoroaster, whose name later was given to the religious movement begun by his father. Cayce's own deep connection to the Christ soul is further revealed in the statement that Zend was one of Uhjltd's two sons from this ancient Persia period. The other was Ujndt, who became as talented in secular leadership as his brother was in spiritual leadership.

The time frame for this story was given in one reading as being somewhere between "seven to ten thousand years B.C." (962-1) On another occasion, a fifteen-year-old boy was told that he had been a son of the wealthy ruler, Croesus, the king of Lydia, who had gathered together a great deal of the world's gold for himself. When asked about the dates of that incarnation, Cayce replied that the "experience was some eight fifty-eight (858)

B.C." (870-1) Later, Gladys Davis amended the reading, suggesting that she had either erred in taking dictation or that Cayce had misstated the date, which was actually 8058 B.C., as corroborated by other references in the readings about the same time period. Whatever the reason, the date for the Uhjltd period in Persia thereafter was considered to be approximately 8000 B.C.

The fact that a number of the names given by Cayce coincide with historical personages who are dated much more recently by modern historians was never problematic where the readings were concerned. For example, as in the case of Croesus, who is generally dated from approximately 560 B.C., the readings suggest that there had been a long line of Persian rulers in an earlier period who had also taken the name Croesus (1265-1). In addition, the readings don't contradict anything from recorded history describing the story of Persia. Instead, rather than detailing simply one period in the history of the world, when Persia was a focal point of civilization, the readings describe two, the first one taking place many millennia prior to the one recorded by history.

One example of a traditional story discussed in the readings is the story of Xerxes, also known in the Bible as Ahasuerus, who ruled Persia in the fifth century B.C. According to the biblical account, during an enormous banquet, the ruler summoned his wife, Vashti, and demanded that she disrobe and show her naked beauty to his drunken guests. When she refused, she was deposed as queen and eventually replaced by a Hebrew maiden named Esther. The story is recounted in the readings because the souls who had once been Vashti and Esther had apparently incarnated as contemporaries of Edgar Cayce, and both received life readings in 1936: cases 1096-1 and 1298-1, respectively. The readings also state that Vashti's reluctance to follow her husband's command was due, in large part, to her strong Zoroastrian beliefs.

A major boost to Cayce's story of ancient Persia occurred in the 1970s, when a series of expeditions to Iran (1972, 1973, 1975, and 1978) were launched by people associated with the A.R.E., for the express purpose of finding remnants of Is-Shlan-doen. Bill and Elsie Sechrist, who served as international representatives for the A.R.E. until their respective deaths in 1987 and 1992, undertook the first trip, accompanied by Ed Jamail, an A.R.E. member from Texas.

The Sechrists met Edgar Cayce in the 1940s. Both received readings, and each was told of their involvement in the history of Is-Shlan-doen. Bill, a successful businessman, was informed in his reading that, during the Persian period, he conducted a caravan from India to Egypt and stopped in the city in the hills and the plains, eventually becoming a resident and establishing a trading post. Elsie's reading informed her that she escaped a life of slavery in India and sought refuge and knowledge in the city. At the time, she had been a kind of seer, able to read both the sands and the stars. In that lifetime, she became one of the more prominent nurses in the healing center established there. The information seemed relevant because Elsie was trained as a nurse in the present and was also extremely skilled with dream interpretation. In fact, she wrote *Dreams—Your Magic Mirror* (1968) and appeared on the *Mike Douglas Show* several times, demonstrating her aptitude with dreams.

In a lecture given in 1979, Bill Sechrist described how, on one of their trips to the area, they pinpointed the location of a cave that they believed contained the ancient remains of Uhjltd. Since Cayce had mentioned that the cave was located seven and one-quarter miles from Shushtar, they decided that one of the first orders of business was to pinpoint the center of town in 1923, when Cayce had first given the reference. According to locals, that location corresponded to a structure called the Friday Mosque. Next, Bill and Elsie got help from a friend who worked for an oil company and had a helicopter at his disposal. Using the computerized guidance system aboard the helicopter, seven and one-quarter miles were mapped out in a southwesterly direction, ranging somewhere between 220 and 230 degrees. Interestingly enough, within that location was found terrain that matched Cayce's description of the topography around Is-Shlan-doen. By Bill's recollection, although the area was only a distance of seven and one-quarter miles away by air, the actual trip to the location took more than eighteen miles by land.

The site was a rolling plain with a deep ravine, apparently cut into the land by water over the intervening years. Without even excavating, the group could see that the ravine was filled with artifacts. Many small mounds that might have been the disintegrated remnants of manmade structures also surrounded the area. Once the Sechrists arrived at the site, Elsie felt as if she were having a past-life recollection and pinpointed the location of the cave to a rocky outcrop in the distance. Later, the group climbed to the place that she believed to be the site of the cave: a huge hole filled with years of debris. According to Ed Jamail, that location was somewhere near latitude 32°N and longitude 48.7°E in southern Iran.

The excitement of their initial discovery led to two subsequent trips by Hugh Lynn Cayce and a return trip by the Sechrists in 1978. During their second trip, Elsie and Bill obtained the cooperation of the chief of geologic studies for the area. They also found a Japanese company ready to finance an excavation. Unfortunately, various uprisings within the country during the transition period between the deposing of the shah and the establishment of an Islamic republic under the Ayatollah Khomeini made any further exploration of the area impossible. After the deaths of Hugh Lynn Cayce and the

The site of the 1972 trip that included Elsie and Bill Sechrist and Ed Jamail.

Hugh Lynn Cayce led a subsequent trip to the area.

Sechrists the impetus to discover the city of Is-Shlandoen seemed all but forgotten.

The next examination of the Uhjltd information appeared with the publication of W.H. Church's *Many Happy Returns* (1984), which explored much of the past-life information given specifically for Edgar Cayce. The book eventually was reissued under the title *The Lives of Edgar Cayce.* Information describing the Persian story as it related to Zend next appeared in Glenn Sanderfur's *Lives of the Master* (1988), which explored the incarnations for Jesus that had been discussed in the Cayce readings. Also planned in the 1980s was a volume in the Edgar Cayce Library Series that was supposed to detail the entire Persian story. The Library Series—verbatim reading extracts on specific topics—had previously explored the story of Egypt in two volumes, and a companion publication on Persia seemed logical. However, the original plans for the Library Series were scaled back, and the Persian volume was never published. Thankfully, Elaine Hruska, of the A.R.E. Press's editorial staff, held on to the extracts, providing a valuable resource for the compilation of this information.

In its entirety, what is most impressive about the Persian myth and the Edgar Cayce material is the cohesiveness of a story that was woven together over a twenty-year period in more than 600 different readings. That story details a flourishing society that began a healing and spiritual ministry in the Iranian desert that would have an impact upon the world even thousands of years later. In part, that impact was shown in several people's life readings, in terms of their ability to see how patterns and experiences from the past became the basis for their activities and relationships in the present. That impact was also felt in Cayce's work as a whole, for his work in the Cayce incarnation was seen, essentially, as a continuation of similar work he had begun in ancient Persia, as well as in ancient Egypt 2,000 years before that. Finally, the impact was felt in a spiritual philosophy that laid the groundwork for Zoroastrianism, perhaps the world's oldest continuous monotheistic religious movement.

This book has been compiled in an effort to bring Cayce's story of ancient Persia to the public. In addition to providing individuals with an overview of the tale, the people, and the civilization with which they were involved, it is hoped that one day some archaeological evidence of Is-Shlan-doen might be discovered. That discovery would give validation to the story woven together by the readings and provide additional verification of Edgar Cayce's ability to somehow peer clearly into the past. Perhaps the evidence exists even now and is simply waiting to be found in a cave, located among the hills and the plains, approximately seven and one-quarter miles southwest of the city of Shushtar in present-day Iran.

1

Notable Events in the Traditional Account of Persian History

History traces the development of the Persian Empire to a hardy people who came from the grasslands of Central Asia and settled between the Caspian Sea and the Persian Gulf. The people called themselves "Irani" and their homeland "Irania" (today known as Iran). In time, they came to be called "Persians" because of the Greeks who named them after their one-time capital of Parsargadae.

Although various legends, mythic history, and the Zend-Avesta (the Zoroastrian Bible) date the earliest periods of the Persian people to approximately 4000 B.C., little is known about the region until the rule of the Median period (approximately 700 B.C.). What came to be called Persia was actually the combined regions of Media, Elam, Chaldea, Babylonia, Assyria, and portions of Arabia, Armenia, and Egypt.

The ancient Persians were known for raising livestock in the mountainous regions of their country and for the cultivation of agriculture in the valleys and the plains. Generally, the founding of the Persian Empire is dated to Cyrus the Great who, in 550 B.C., conquered the Medes and acquired Assyria, then conquered Lydia, which had been ruled by the historical Croesus I. The history of Persia is often divided into five dynastic periods dating from this conquest: the Armenian Dynasty, beginning with Cyrus and ending with the conquest of Alexander the Great (550-331 B.C.); the Greek or Seleucian Dynasty, named for one of Alexander's generals (331-250 B.C.); the Parthian Dynasty (250 B.C.-227 A.D.); the Sassanian Dynasty (A.D. 227-651); and the Islamic period (A.D. 651 to the present).

The prominence of historic Persia in the history of the world can be dated from the death of King Nebuchadnezzar, ruler of Babylon. After his death, the Babylonian Empire was divided into three regions: Babylon, Lydia, and Media. Cyrus became king of Media and eventually conquered the other two kingdoms. In time, he built his capital city in Parsargadae. By 539 B.C., Croesus I added Babylon and Palestine to his conquests, at which time he allowed the Jews to return from the Babylonian exile that had been imposed upon them by King Nebuchadnezzar more than sixty years previously. Because of Cyrus, the Jews were able to return to their homeland and rebuild the temple in Jerusalem that had been destroyed by Nebuchadnezzar.

After his conquest of Babylon, Cyrus attempted to expand his empire into India. He was killed in a battle with eastern nomads in 529 B.C. and was buried in his capital city. For the next seven years, Cyrus's son, Cambyses II, took control of the empire and conquered the Sinai Peninsula and Egypt. Later, because of various claims to the throne, he either committed suicide or was killed. Several portions of Cyrus's empire began to revolt. In 522 B.C., Darius, a distant cousin of Cambyses II, seized the crown for himself, did away with any other claimants to the throne, and began to systematically reclaim the empire.

History suggests that the Zoroastrian faith existed from approximately 600 B.C., beginning with the activities of the prophet Zarathustra, also called Zoroaster by the Greeks, who began proselytizing in the northwest portion of the country. However, some rare Zoroastrian texts actually place the date many thousands of years earlier, to approximately 7500 B.C.[3] Some Zoroastrians, who often call themselves Parsees, suggest that this wide variance in dates is due to the fact that there was not one Zarathustra but three. The first was a Sumerian philosopher who lived about 7000 B.C. The second was an Iranian teacher who compiled an encyclopedia of the earlier traditions. The third was a Median priest who revived the half-forgotten teachings of his predecessors. Nonetheless, traditional history dates Zarathustra from approximately 660 to 583 B.C. Apparently, Zarathustra began receiving his revelations when he was still a young man.

Although the Persian king, Cyrus, was a worshiper of the many Babylonian nature gods, a number of his successors embraced Zoroastrianism. In fact, the Zoroastrian faith received a major push with the conversion of Vishtaspa, a king in the eastern portion of the country, by Zarathustra himself. This conversion proved invaluable

---

[3]*A Manual of Khshnoom: The Zoroastrian Occult Knowledge,* by Phiroz Nasaevanji Tavaria, States People Press, Bombay, 1971; and *Life of Ustab Saheb Behramshah Nowroji Shroff,* by Meher Master-Moos, Mazdayasnie Monasterie, Bombay, 1981.

in the flourishing of the faith because Vishtaspa happened to be the father of Darius, who took control of the empire in 522 B.C. The religion preached by Zarathustra prospered and, eventually, Plato, Aristotle, and other Greek thinkers showed great interest in his doctrines.

Unlike some of the mystery religions that were open only to certain classes of people, the religion of Zarathustra was open to all. According to his teachings, there was one supreme God, known as Ahura Mazda. In spite of the supremacy of this one God, there was also a spirit of evil and darkness, called Ahriman, with whom Ahura Mazda was in conflict. Because humanity could choose to align itself with either good or evil, the Zoroastrian faith championed the purity of body, mind, and soul and exhorted believers to "good thoughts, good words, good deeds." Converts to the faith were expected to exert unwavering care in their respect for the elements of earth, water, and fire, and to never be the cause of the defilement of those elements in any way. Virtues such as generosity, kindness, honesty, truth, and respect were to be cultivated by all. Marriage to other converts of the faith was encouraged, as was the raising of children. The faith bears a striking resemblance to both Judaism and Christianity in its belief in angels and archangels, the coming of a Messiah, the resurrection of the dead, the eventual establishment of a perfect kingdom, and everlasting life.

Although Darius appeared open to other faiths, he apparently adopted at least some of his father's beliefs from the Zoroastrian religion. It was under Darius that the Persian Empire entered its golden age, solidified its borders, and saw much prosperity. Darius divided his empire into a system of twenty provinces, each led by a provincial governor. Under a system of taxation and military support, each province was responsible for providing the empire with soldiers, as well as an annual tribute. To encourage commerce, Darius standardized coins, weights, and measures; built imperial highways; and created an irrigation and canal system from the Nile to the Red Sea. Under his leadership, the empire operated smoothly for twenty years, until 500 B.C., when the Greek cities in Asia Minor rebelled. Darius put down the rebellion and then tried to conquer Athens in retaliation for its role in aiding the rebel cities. He was beaten in the battle of Marathon, and a subsequent follow-up assault came to an end in 486 B.C. with his death.

After Darius's death, his son, Xerxes, took control of the empire. History knows Xerxes primarily through his reputation as weak and tyrannical, as well as for his role in the book of Esther under the name Ahasuerus. His twenty-year reign, from 486 to 465 B.C., saw the first signs of decay in the empire when his army experienced defeat by some of the Greek city-states that had been controlled by his father. Xerxes was eventually murdered at Persepolis by the captain of his palace guard, and for the next 125 years, Persian history was filled with conspiracies, assassinations, and the revolt of various portions of the empire.

Although the empire briefly was reunited under the cruelty of Artaxerxes III (359 to 338 B.C.), who killed many of his own relatives to assure the stability of his reign, Artaxerxes himself was eventually killed. A few years later, Darius III (336 to 330 B.C.) was on the throne when Alexander the Great led his powerful armies into Asia.

Alexander the Great (356-323 B.C.) became king of Macedonia in 336 B.C. after the assassination of his father. Within two years, he began his war against Persia, defeating a Persian army near the ancient city of Troy. Afterward, all the states of Asia Minor submitted to his rule. Alexander continued his advances, defeating the main Persian army, led by Darius III, at Issus in 333 B.C.

Darius escaped but was beaten again in 331 B.C. when Babylon surrendered. Shortly after, Darius III was killed by one of his own followers, and Alexander moved his forces toward Persepolis, the Persian capital, finally conquering and taking control of what remained of the Persian Empire.

In order to tighten his control on the empire, Alexander founded dozens of Greek and Macedonian colonies throughout Persia. He and his armies also did much to stamp out the Zoroastrian faith and, according to legend, even managed to destroy the only original copies of the Zend-Avesta that remained. In the spring of 323 B.C., Alexander contracted a fever and died, leaving the fate of the empire to be decided among his generals, including Seleucus I, who proved victorious among various contenders and founded the Seleucid dynasty. For the next fifty years, rivalry between the Macedonians and the Greeks, as well as between Seleucus's heirs and sons, caused fractures within the empire, culminating with Parthia being freed from Macedonian rule in 250 B.C.

The Parthian Dynasty in Persia lasted from 250 B.C. to approximately A.D. 227. What is most notable about that period are the various wars that the Parthians had with Rome, often proving to be Rome's superior in battle. In one famous battle between Marc Antony and the Parthian king, Phraates, the Parthians defeated the Romans in spite of the fact that they numbered only 40,000 against a Roman army of at least 100,000! Because of the Parthian might, for more than 100 years, Rome dared not risk another attack against Parthia. During the Parthian Dynasty, the Zoroastrian faith also experienced a rebirth, attracting new converts to the movement. The dynasty came to an end in A.D. 227, when King Vologeses V was defeated and put to death by Ardashir, founder of the Sassanian Dynasty.

During the Sassanian period, the Persian nation tried

repeatedly to enforce its old claims on western Asia. Battles against Rome, Syria, Mesopotamia, and Antioch were fought in an attempt to reestablish portions of the empire, with only partial success. The empire also expanded into Armenia and India. Under the Sassanian Dynasty, Zoroastrianism became the official religion and, for a time, anyone leaving the faith was subject to punishment by death. Although no original copies of the complete Zend-Avesta existed, fragments had been pieced together in order to disseminate the faith. After A.D. 275, another Zoroastrianism revival began. Some of the Sassanid kings of this period became intolerant of all other religions and began persecuting anyone deemed to be heathen, Christian, or a follower of Manichaeism (a religion which promoted the dualistic philosophy of good and evil). The Christians experienced a brief period of freedom under the reign of Yezdegerd (A.D. 399 to 420), who had married a Jewish woman. Christianity was allowed to spread, and churches were permitted to be built, but the persecution began anew with the death of Yezdegerd in A.D. 420.

Zoroastrianism remained the national faith of Persia after that period. However, various kings proclaimed periods of toleration of other faiths, including Chosroes (A.D. 531-579), who reportedly married a Christian woman and whose own son was said to have converted to Christianity. His successor, Chosroes II, took advantage of the weakening Byzantine Empire and expanded the Persian Empire back into Syria, Antioch, Palestine, and Alexandria. The end came when Chosroes II demanded that the daughter of a Christian Arab be his wife, in spite of the fact that he reportedly already had 3,000 wives. The Arab, named Na'aman, refused to permit his Christian daughter to enter the harem of a Zoroastrian. As a result, he was killed, provoking the scattered Arab tribes to revolt against the empire. Chosroes II was defeated in the revolt. In time, his successor, Yezdegerd III, also was defeated by Muslim Arabs, bringing an end to the Sassanian Dynasty.

In A.D. 641 Khalif Omar subjugated Persia to the Islamic faith and incorporated the empire into his caliphate. Those who resisted conversion to Islam and who managed to escape eventually found their way to India. Today, some 150,000 Zoroastrians live in India, most of them in Bombay. For the next 1,000 years, the history of Persia was marked by periods of invasion, civil war, conquest, defeat, and the establishment of various principalities and short-lived dynasties. In the mid-eleventh century, the Seljuk Turks conquered the country, followed by the Mongols and the Turkomans over the next 400 years.

The Turkomans were overthrown by Ismail I, who proclaimed himself shah, founded the Safavid Dynasty (A.D. 1501-1722), and established Shiite doctrine as the official religion. The Safavids were overthrown in A.D. 1722 by the Afghan army and, afterward, Russia and Turkey attempted to divide the country but ultimately failed in their plan.

The nineteenth and early twentieth centuries witnessed a struggle between Britain and Russia for ultimate control of Persia. After World War I, the government changed the name from Persia to its more ancient name of Iran. Allied troops occupied the area throughout World War II in order to protect the rich oil fields from possible German seizure. During the 1950s, a political crisis developed over the oil industry. The shah negotiated a lucrative agreement from the Arab oil consortium that guaranteed Iran a favorable profit margin and brought economic prosperity to the region. The shah began to exercise greater control over the government and, eventually, faced widespread opposition from conservatives who wanted the country governed by Islamic law and those who believed the shah had stolen much of the country's wealth. Riots eventually led to the shah fleeing abroad in 1979, where he died a few years later.

After the revolt, the Ayatollah Khomeini, a Muslim clergyman who had been living in exile, returned to the country and established an Islamic republic. After Khomeini's death in 1989, Iran's relations with the West improved because of President Ali Akbar Hashemi Rafsanjani's role in obtaining the release of Western hostages held in Lebanon. In 1997, Mohammed Khatami, who had served as a minister of cultural affairs under both Khomeini and Rafsanjani, was named president. Khatami became known for his advocacy of political reform and his belief in the freedom of the press.

Today, the country includes religious conservatives as well as those who consider themselves more progressive and interested in dealing with the Western world.

2

The Early History of Ancient Persia Before the City of Is-Shlan-doen

Centuries before the Persia of Cyrus, Darius, and Xerxes, ancient nomadic tribes roamed the Arab lands. These wandering people lived in animal-skin tents or in caves, under very primitive conditions. They were forced to deal with much hardship, a lack of water, and border skirmishes with and raids from those of other tribes. Filth and disease were the all-too-common ingredients of desert life.

In the face of such adversity, a world of plenty seems hard to fathom, and yet, there were prosperous cities and rulers who somehow managed to thrive. The existence of gold, spices, jewelry, and various other trade commodities encouraged the development of trade routes among numerous cities. These same riches also gave rise to the proliferation of desert bandits and thieving nomads. Caravans were frequently plundered, and no one was a more favored target than King Croesus II, one in a long line of Persian rulers who somehow managed to create a fortified kingdom along a portion of the Persian frontier.

Famed for his wealth and his abuse of power, Croesus II established a prized city, a legendary treasury, and a training school for maidens where the daughters of wealthy citizens were educated in culture and the proper place of a nobleman's wife. He was also known for his raids in retaliation for the raids against him. Croesus frequently ordered battles against the scattered desert people beyond the borders of his kingdom, supplementing his tremendous wealth in the process.

In addition to uprisings against Croesus, there was ongoing conflict among the nomadic tribes. It was a time when the land was divided and warfare was common among the various peoples. Tribes often attacked one another or rioted against their own leaders. The looting of cattle and livestock was a way of life and, often, the only means of survival. Captives (especially women) were frequently taken and eventually assimilated into rival settlements. Spying was a common occurrence among tribes and desert kingdoms. Much of the conflict overran the Persian countryside, a place of rolling hills and wide-open desert expanses.

During the course of a reading given in 1934, Edgar Cayce informed a twenty-year-old man that, in a previous life, the man had been among the nomads in ancient Persia who continually warred with one another. From that experience, he learned to adapt himself to a variety of people and cultures—a strength he retained in the present. At the same time, however, he apparently acquired a strong sense of self-preservation, as well as a tendency toward depression and personal melancholy:

The entity then was among those that went, or desired to act in the capacity of the spy for those peoples that would raid upon the Persian or Lydian group; in those periods when there was much to be accomplished by raids one upon another.

In the present experience such would be called banditry, yet in those sojourns much that we would give in the present as taking advantage of the abilities in education in any line of endeavor was the same consideration of such activities, and they were not looked upon as being robbery or banditry in that experience.

Yet the entity, as we have indicated, from the innate activity, was one that could (and can in the present) act in the capacity of taking advantage of the situations by the abilities to communicate, associate, speak with and address self in such a manner as to undermine the better of those that sought to prevent such associations.

Then in the name Udlden, the entity lost and gained; for being in the periods when the dissensions arose soon after the return of spying out of the land, there was brought dissension and much of that sullenness which is manifested within self in the present—which brought about the separation of the entity from those peoples, and was lost in the attempt to create or bring about those activities with others in more distant lands. 568-1

In response to the warring nomads, a number of Persian kings and wealthy merchants banded together and hired soldiers and mercenary patrols in order to ensure the continuation of their commercial activities. At the time, trade routes existed between Persia and such lands as India, Egypt, the Ukraine, and the Macedonian lands (eventually known as Greece, Bulgaria, and Yugoslavia).

The control which these kings and members of the aristocracy attempted to place upon the nomadic tribes was often oppressive. In addition to preventing attacks on trade caravans, the activities of the soldiers and the mercenary forces often prevented the desert people from going about their normal activities and their way of life. These attempts at confinement caused the nomadic tribes to rebel all the more.

Tribal leaders were responsible for the survival of their people. The most gifted made powerful adversaries, ensuring the continuity of their reign and the perseverance of their settlements. However, tribal leadership was not a lifetime appointment. Leaders who were weak or self-serving did not last. Rival factions within the tribe eventually replaced leaders who proved more interested in their own sustenance or in the acquisition of personal wealth than in the needs of their people. Tribal instability and short-lived allegiances among various tribes became normal components of desert life.

According to the Cayce readings, among these nomadic rulers was a leader of the tribe of Zu, named Eujueltd. Apparently his desert people formed an alliance with the tribe of Ra, a group distantly related to the Egyptians. It was hoped that the unification of these two tribes might somehow bring together the strength of Egypt and strength of the desert.

In 1934, a fifty-seven-year-old man received a reading and was advised: "In giving that which may be helpful for the entity in its present development, much of every nature crowds in to be told; for the pages that are written, the influences that have borne upon the activities of the entity are many." (707-1) One of those influences from the past was his incarnation as Eujueltd, when he had taken as his companion Slumdki, a woman from the tribe of Ra, in order to further bond the alliance between the two tribes. Interestingly enough, four years earlier, the woman who had been Slumdki also received a life reading. The information she received highlighted her numerous abilities in understanding human relationships:

Teacher

> One appreciative of abilities in others. Also the abilities to make friendships; to pass judgment on individual, group and classes, making for those influences in mental as a teacher—rather by the example, than by precept; not influencing individuals or groups through word of mouth, but rather by the influence of application of self in their experience, their lives; weighing often those influences in individuals' lives, bringing for others the understandings of themselves, in the manner of judgement *for* themselves. Living and letting live. Not using those influences for selfish motives, but rather that individuals may *apply* themselves in that which for the individual will bring the understanding. 2708-1

Baby":
Create
Child Attract
Soul ion
by Ideals

After coming together as companions—what would be called husband and wife in the present—the couple decided to serve their joint tribes in the greatest fashion they could imagine. With that in mind, the readings say, Eujueltd and Slumdki purposefully chose to serve as the parental channels for a great soul. Their joint desire was to have a child who might somehow aid in bringing peace to the desert. With that as their ideal, the couple conceived and had a son they named Uhjltd. The two shared their hopes for this child with others within the tribe, and it was generally agreed that, when the time was right, this Uhjltd would become the leader of their combined settlements.

The readings state that, after the birth of Uhjltd, Eujueltd and Slumdki had additional children. Unfortunately, for some reason, Eujueltd soon forgot the idealistic principles that had led him to desire to father a great soul at the birth of his first son. The additional children who came to the couple, Uhjltd's brothers and sisters, did not possess the same level of soul strengths as their elder brother. A second son, named Oujida, was born to the couple and became very much a part of nomadic life. In time, he became his father's favorite and a leader in his own right among the warriors of the tribe.

In the beginning, Uhjltd was raised as any young Persian nomad. He learned to survive in the desert. He learned to tame wild horses and to ride them. He also learned to take part in the attacks on small caravans and the occasional border skirmishes into Croesus's fabled territory. Uhjltd and his siblings grew to adulthood as members of the combined tribes of Ra and Zu. Uhjltd was often referred to as the settlement's future leader, apparently causing some measure of sibling rivalry with his brother, Oujida.

Whether it was in response to an attack from Croesus or because Oujida and his fellow warriors became careless and arrogant in their thirst for battle, the day came when Uhjltd's brother and a band of men decided to attack Croesus's kingdom for themselves. Without discussing the matter with other members of the settlement, they attacked the famed temple school that was rumored to be inhabited by the most beautiful women in all the king's vast territories. Evidently, such an assault within the very heart of Croesus's kingdom had never been imagined, and the tribal warriors were able to enter the city, taking spoils from the treasury as well as the maidens they sought.

In 1928, the parents of a five-year-old girl were informed that their daughter had been among the temple maidens and had surrendered her life in defense of Croesus's daughter. As a result, in the twentieth-century life, she was slow in making friendships but extremely committed to them once they were established (38-1). On another occasion, a twenty-seven-year-old woman learned that she had also been among the school maidens, losing her life in the assault as well:

> The entity then in that school in which the destructive forces were brought, and in the massacre did the entity lose the life, and then in the name Mjhel, and the dread as is innate in the entity of firearms and of weapons, from or in the hands of others, and especially of knives or large swords; yet in *own* hands ever ready to use same. 2692-1

As soon as the surviving women were captured and strapped to horses or held on horseback by the mounted warriors, Oujida and his men returned to their settlement. Two things had occurred during the invasion of the temple school that neither Oujida nor his men had foreseen: Several maidens had been killed in the assault, and among the captives was Elia, the king's own daughter, whom the warriors had taken.

To make matters worse, during the journey from the temple school back to the nomad's settlement, a few of the girls were raped, and at least one decided to take her life rather than stay a captive. It was on the return to his settlement that Oujida discovered that Croesus's daughter, Elia, was one of the captives. Apparently as a means of appeasing his brother's anger for having undertaken the raid in the first place, Oujida decided to offer Elia to Uhjltd as his share of the booty. It was an offering that Uhjltd refused, prompting Oujida to take Elia as his own wife—much to the woman's dismay, for in addition to being taken from her people, her status had fallen from princess and daughter of a king to wife of a desert nomad.

Somehow, the nomad settlement survived a counterattack from Croesus's forces, and life went on. Although it is not mentioned in the Cayce readings, perhaps that battle was the impetus that sent Uhjltd to Egypt for his training as the eventual ruler. He no doubt needed the wisdom and knowledge of the ancients if he were to lead his people beyond the meager existence they had come to know. In Egypt, Uhjltd learned a great deal. Apparently, he also "relearned" many of the same things he had once known firsthand, during an earlier incarnation as an Egyptian high priest named Ra Ta. While Uhjltd was away, tribal life within the settlement of Ra and Zu continued much the same.

At the same time, however, Oujida's jealousy continued and was reinforced by the fact that several members of the tribe began to wonder aloud whether Oujida might not be the best one to lead the people after all.

After Oujida took Elia to be his wife, she soon became pregnant and gave birth to a baby girl, who was named Inxa. Rather than being delighted with the birth of her child, Elia grew even more depressed. There appeared no way she could return to the life she had once known. Because of her depression and her hatred of the man who had captured her, Elia committed suicide rather than remaining among the desert nomads. She plunged a knife into her breast when her child was still an infant; the little girl was left with Oujida and raised with contempt for her uncle, Uhjltd.

In 1927, Edgar Cayce informed a twenty-two-year-old woman that she had been Elia, daughter to Croesus II. Although she had gained in soul development during the early portion of that lifetime, her act of suicide had caused her to regress, forcing her to face the same level of depression in the present. Her reading advised her, "The entity lost through this experience, to the detriment of self, to the low dreg that of taking life in the way to satisfy self; not in defense of principle or of self, country or position . . . " (369-3)

During Uhjltd's absence in Egypt, tribal warfare among various groups and occasional skirmishes with Croesus continued. Croesus's controlling temperament came to light in 1944, when a reading advised a thirty-two-year-old sheet-metal worker that he had been Croesus II and that he still allowed the authority he had been vested with in the earlier life often to become abusive in this one. In the present, he also had a difficult time controlling his temper. Both of these tendencies had been cultivated during his lifetime in ancient Persia, a time when he had been "a hard-hearted guy, with more power than he used properly." (5001-1) He had apparently been responsible for much of the repression directed against the nomadic tribes.

In addition to raids and warring patrols, some of that repression came in the form of taxation, for Croesus employed several people for the express purpose of analyzing "the abilities of the peoples of the various lands— as to how, in what manner, in what form, tax or payments for the upkeep of the land might be best brought from the varied groups." (2533-1) Croesus's treasury grew because of his ongoing attempts to tax the tribes throughout the eastern portion of the country, all the way to the shores of the Great Sea.

Revenues were also generated by commercial activities. The kingdom served as a stopping point along the various trade routes. In addition to wealthy merchants and the temple school for the training of maidens, Croesus's court included physicians, soldiers, record keepers, mediators, advisors, keepers of the treasury, even astrologers and soothsayers, whose keep required great sums of money. In 1935, Edgar Cayce told a forty-year-old banker that he had been among the members of Croesus II's court, as well as in the court of Croesus's father:

The entity then was among the keepers of the

treasury during the first and second Croesus; for this was among the *early* experiences, being some seven to ten thousand years B.C.

And in this activity the entity rose to pomp, to power, and not always used properly.

In that experience the entity, in the name Ixelte, gained and lost . . .

From that experience arises in the present the desire of those things of an oriental touch about the entity; especially as to hangings, draperies or rugs. These have a peculiar influence upon the entity, as an innate urge—or one that arises from those influences through which the entity passed when it was a judge of many such things. 962-1

A sixteen-year-old student learned that he had also served Croesus as a counselor and advisor. A past-life reading stated that the boy's interest in people in positions of power and authority originated from that same period:

The entity then was among the Persian peoples, being closely associated with the king (Croesus) of that period; for the entity was—not what later became termed as the armor bearer, but—rather the advisor, the counselor to the king, or being one upon whom the king depended oft for the making known as to the activities of those who had been given missions to perform; not as a spy, but as one acting in the capacity of a counselor—not one of whom those who were commissioned were afraid, but one with whom they most yearned or desired to counsel through those experiences.

Thus we find in the present the entity's interest in, or the latent urges for, those things having to do with individuals in power, or those in places in which there is the ability to counsel those of all classes of individuals in their seeking out of ways and means for men to dwell together better in a unity or harmony as a nation. Yet, nationalism is not that most manifested, but something just between that *and* the privileges of the individual in relationship to same.

Then the entity was in the name Esdresen. 2285-1

Another former member of Croesus II's court was a fifty-one-year-old librarian who received a reading in 1944. Her present-day interest in mysticism and various states of consciousness was traced to the Persian period, when her name was Shamgar and she was one of the king's soothsayers:

Before that we find the entity was in the Persian land during those periods when there were those activities in the "city in the hills and the plains." The entity then was a soothsayer in the courts of Croesus and a student of the mysteries of the east and of the sands, and the relationships of stars with the earth. For all, as the entity held and yet fully not interpreted but in the present finds, are of one source; and that which forms brilliancy of the star, in the morning star, is that which also may be the dullness as from the earth itself, but reflecting that which is the source of light shines out to others. 5149-1

After Uhjltd's educational period in Egypt, which might have encompassed many years, the time finally arrived for him to return to the land of his birth. His experiences in Egypt returned him to his people a changed man. Many among Uhjltd's old tribe were not eager to accept the changes that had occurred in him. Their own ways of life had become much too ingrained, and they had no firsthand experience with Uhjltd's education or his transformational experiences in Egypt. Many among the tribesmen believed they might be better served by following Oujida, for Uhjltd's younger brother kept to their old ways. Still, some of the older tribesmen remained hopeful that Uhjltd would be able to lead the people of the combined tribes of Ra and Zu to a better way of life.

During the 1930s, when a movie telling the story of ancient Persia was being contemplated, Edgar Cayce was asked to describe the scene that took place after Uhjltd's return from Egypt. He responded:

There was awe, consternation, in the feelings and the minds of many as they waited expectantly for the return of him whom all felt was destined to unite the factions of the tribesmen. The anxiety of the sages had been heightened by the revolt again and again of the younger men of the two factions, but the day had arrived when many of these had united in going to meet their leader, Uhjltd; for he was returning from the land of Ra, his mother's land, that day.

So, when the guard had signaled, there was evidence of the approach of those long looked for. Excitement soon ran throughout the camp, and all gathered in the common meeting ground between the factions' camps.

He made an imposing figure on his cream colored charger, as he rode among those who in eager expectation were wont to make all character of suggestions as to what the changes would be, once he was accepted and declared leader of his clan. Many told of the numbers that would rally to the clan under the leadership of the younger man. Tall, straight, heavy brow, with piercing gray eyes, he presented a picture *worthy* of calling the attention of all. With easy mien, yet seemingly hearing and answering every one in such a manner as to cause the old, the young, the fiery, the sedate, to feel they were being heard by indeed a master, a figure among men.

As he approaches and is received by the older men, then goes apart for the moment with those of his own household, there was consternation and awe, yet all in reverence, as to what might be expected the course this man was to give this at once a united peoples.

When this was settled, or changes came, he was proclaimed their chief, their leader, their dependent one, and the course of events as in keeping with the regulations of the tribes he graciously accepts, and sets apart his tent and is immediately besieged by young and old that he is to choose a mate from among those of his own peoples. These he graciously puts aside in one form or another, without causing any particular disturbance or distrust in the mind of any.

In the days that follow there begin then the reports that are made by the various runners, or outposts and leaders to this commander or chief, as to the activities of the peoples. He, Uhjltd, attempts to—by setting up the intercourse of exchange of those things in one portion of that kingdom overseen or run by him and his peoples for that in other lands. This succeeds in part, and there is built up something of an understanding that is satisfactory to many of the older ones, yet raids are sought by many of the younger peoples. These are held in check by the leader himself, his reprimands becoming rather as befriending those that would lead off or disobey orders. 294-144

Almost immediately upon assuming his leadership role, Uhjltd began making various changes in the activities of his tribal settlement. When asked to discuss what changes Uhjltd made, Cayce replied:

inner qualities reflect outward ways

> The difference in the outlook, or the civic conditions about the camp, the _cleanliness_—that is easily shown, as well as the _order_ that comes out of practically chaos; the arising for the morning and evening prayer, the gathering in _orderly_ form; as well as the accoutrements through which the aid is brought, and the manner in which aid is brought, to individuals in the caravans, or conducting of caravans through the country—see? 294-145

ORDER

DO RIGHT

From that time on, Uhjltd's motivation for himself and his people became simply to "*Dare* ever to do right in the face of all circumstances!"

Uhjltd's new way of dealing with his own people and other tribes proved problematic for some. Although the tribe of Ra and Zu was ordered to stop their assaults on rival territories and the kingdom of Croesus, the tribe continued to face attacks from others. Uhjltd's settlement became the target of frequent invasion, but he approved assaults against others only in response to such attacks. This approach caused more and more people within the tribe to dispute their leader's wisdom. Even Uhjltd's siblings and his father began to question his leadership. Dissension, disorder, and internal conflict became more widespread. Many among the younger warriors longed for the old ways of life. Still, Uhjltd was adamant in his desire for peace.

Uhjltd came to believe that, between the continuous fighting with neighboring tribes and the ongoing skirmishes with Croesus, the entire settlement would eventually be destroyed unless something was done. If things did not change, his people were doomed. For that reason, Uhjltd decided to put an end to the rivalry himself. After pondering his options, he decided upon an unheard-of course of action. In an effort to achieve peace with Croesus's kingdom, he decided to journey to the kingdom alone and speak with the king as an emissary of peace.

Once his decision was made, Uhjltd called his people together and informed them of what he was going to do. Many wondered about the wisdom of such a plan. Some doubted whether or not Croesus's attacks would ever become more than the periodic raids that they had grown used to. Others may have believed that Uhjltd was simply fleeing the settlement in order to escape the king's wrath. Nonetheless, Uhjltd had made his decision.

In describing the scene that took place when Uhjltd set out on his lone journey upon his prized horse, the Cayce readings say that he left his brother in charge of protecting the tribe. The ruler's departing speech challenged his people to begin living in a new way, one that set aside personal desires and took into account the needs of others. Uhjltd's remarks were the last that many from the tribe ever heard him make, for over the days that followed, the future of the combined settlement of Ra and Zu was completely altered.

After departing from the tribe of his birth and his family, Uhjltd made the solitary journey to Croesus II's kingdom. He appeared as an ordinary nomad, not someone who had been educated in the mysteries of Egypt and ruled an enormous desert settlement. The journey across the desert was long and hard, perhaps several days in duration. The blazing sun and the long stretches of desert sand proved exhausting. It was no wonder that Uhjltd sought relief from his thirst at a well just beyond the walls of Croesus's desert kingdom.

The marvelous image of the desert well—with three

beautiful palm trees soaring high above—made a lasting impression upon the wearied traveler, as did the most beautiful maiden Uhjltd had ever seen, who stood nearby. According to the readings, there was an immediate attraction between the two, even from their first meeting. In fact, these two souls had always been connected in one way or another since their first earthly incarnation: "With the meeting, when each have become so taken, there is the realizing of, or awakening to, the oneness of their souls . . . " (288-6)

In spite of their immediate attraction, however, Uhjltd and the woman, whose name was Ilya, came from two completely different worlds. Ilya's father was Leodin, brother to King Croesus. She was refined and had been educated, along with other daughters of nobles, at the temple school. She had been surrounded with pomp, grandeur, and everything due a member of a royal family. Uhjltd had been raised among the warring tribes of the plains and had been treated as a wanderer and a nomad for much of his life.

Uhjltd was completely taken with Ilya. She set aside the attraction he held for her, however, when she somehow became aware that he was connected to the earlier attack on the temple school. In addition to suffering the deaths of some of her friends and the kidnapping of many more, Ilya was first cousin and close friend to Elia, the princess taken by Oujida. When Ilya realized Uhjltd's identity as the ruler of the same tribesmen who were responsible for crimes against the kingdom, she decided to deceive him.

Because of her beauty and her false portrayal of empathy toward him, Ilya managed to extract from Uhjltd the purpose of his journey. In response, she volunteered that she had some influence with Croesus's court and promised to return the next day, possibly with the offer of an audience with Croesus. Uhjltd was overjoyed with

the offer. It seemed that his decision to make the journey had been correct after all.

As agreed, Uhjltd came to the well at the appointed
hour the very next day. Ilya appeared and escorted him
into the gates of the city. Immediately after entering the
city, however, he was taken prisoner by three guards and
escorted to the prison tower. When Ilya saw the confusion in Uhjltd's eyes because of her deception, she ran
off to her chambers in her own confusion over the mixed
emotions she felt for a man she had only just met. Although Uhjltd was captured and imprisoned, his horse
somehow escaped capture and ran off into the desert.

Apparently the news of Uhjltd's capture and identity
was never taken to Croesus. Instead, Ilya alerted only the
guards, who would decide what was to be done with
their prisoner, a decision about which the guards dis-
agreed. Because of Uhjltd's wisdom, friendly disposition,
and stature, as the days passed many of the guards refused to believe that this man came from one of the nomadic Bedouin tribes. Some claimed he was a holy man;
others, a scholar of stature. A few of the guards even ar-
gued among themselves as to whether Uhjltd had actually been hired by Croesus to infiltrate their ranks and
discern their loyalty to the king.

Somehow, word leaked back to Uhjltd—probably
through one of the guards—that he no longer had a city
to return to. During his short absence, his brother and
some rival factions fought for leadership. The ensuing
struggle broke the tribe into several groups. The group
that followed Oujida was driven into land controlled by
Egypt's Pharaoh, where they hastily made camp.

While he had lost the city of his birth, Uhjltd's stature
among the guards continued to grow. However, no
agreement could be reached as to what was to be done
with this man without a country of his own. Meanwhile,
during the days that followed Uhjltd's imprisonment,

Ilya began to acknowledge second thoughts about having deceived him. She sought out one of her teachers in the temple school, whose name may have been Irenan, and described her involvement in Uhjltd's capture. Because her teacher was an "instructress" of great knowledge, Ilya hoped the woman might be able to comment on or learn the true nature of the prisoner held by the guards.

One reading described the turn of events after Uhjltd's capture this way:

> . . . Uhjltd was then *chained* in the walls of this outpost, both hands and feet, and—as there was the little association or communication—the one that had brought same in, or made for the possible capture of this one—sought, through the efforts of one that was being guarded by the same group, that had been instructress, to know something *of* this leader that had become as a by-word, or—as would be termed in the present—an individual of renown. 294-142

Even while Croesus's guards remained uncertain about what to do with the prisoner, Irenan and Ilya decided that Uhjltd needed to be set free. As luck would have it, one of the prison guards, named Endessoseu, was a friend to Irenan, and he allowed the two women admittance. Evidently, the women had simply requested to see the prisoner for whose capture Ilya had been responsible. During their visit, the two managed to loosen the chains that held Uhjltd pinned to the wall.

Uhjltd managed to escape from the prison immediately. Unfortunately, he was also injured as he fell from the city wall to the desert sands below, hurting his arm and, perhaps, injuring a leg or an ankle in the fall. The readings suggest that his injury occurred somewhere near the same well he had reached when first approaching the city. Whatever the injury, it became clear that outrunning the guards was not possible. Just when Uhjltd believed that recapture seemed inevitable, his horse ran up to greet him. Somehow, the faithful creature had been waiting for signs of his master ever since Uhjltd had first entered the city. Relieved and surprised, Uhjltd climbed on the back of his charger and began to ride from Croesus's kingdom as swiftly as possible. His escape did not go unnoticed, however. Apparently, the involvement of Ilya and Irenan had been witnessed by some of the prison guards:

> In this they were spied upon by those in authority, and for their lack of vigilance—or their seeming or apparent turning to aid that which had brought *about* what would seem to have made for peace— they were cast from the tower. In the escape, as Uhjltd rode on his own dapple charger, or horse, this was seen—and the return for the body that was cast from the tower. 294-142

As he rode away, Uhjltd looked back to see both Ilya and Irenan thrown from the tower, apparently banished from the city because of their traitorous involvement in a prisoner's escape. Without giving the matter a second thought, Uhjltd turned his horse back toward the city and rode as quickly as possible to aid the two women.

When she was thrown from the tower, Irenan was injured. In spite of his own injuries, Uhjltd dismounted his horse and lifted her onto the creature's back. Ilya mounted the horse as well. Just as they were attempting to escape, some of the guards (those who had not come to admire Uhjltd) attempted to stone the three from atop the city wall, causing further injuries to each of the escapees. In the commotion, some of the stones met their mark, knocking Uhjltd to the ground. In great pain, stumbling, and nearly unconscious from the injuries he had received, Uhjltd somehow managed to climb upon the back of his horse with the women, and the three rode off into the desert in search of a place of refuge and safety.

3

The Birth of the City in the Hills and the Plains

Somehow Uhjltd's horse managed to carry the three fugitives across the vast desert plains. The journey was slow, and with neither supplies nor water, the trio's survival beyond a couple of days appeared unlikely. The threat of being followed by Croesus's guards also was real, but the physical condition of the three left them unable to focus on the dangers. Irenan's injuries were so serious that the woman lapsed in and out of consciousness. Uhjltd, too, became more ill with each passing hour. Ilya was in the best condition but, without water, even she could not survive for long. The horse continued its journey away from Croesus's kingdom, toward an unknown destination. The fugitives rested only when the horse was exhausted from their weight, and they resumed their journey as soon as the creature was able.

By dawn of the third day, Irenan and Uhjltd were near death, and Ilya was on the verge of collapse. The horse led them to a place of scattered desert hills and a central cave within which they found cool shelter. Uhjltd and Irenan both fell unconscious. Ilya, however, was aware enough to realize that the moist walls of the cave suggested the presence of water. Descending farther into the cave, she quickly found an underground spring. After quenching her own thirst, she brought water to Uhjltd and Irenan. Although the three were not yet aware of it, the Cayce readings suggest that they had happened onto the remnants of an ancient city that had been "abandoned by some of the offsprings of Cain—in conjunction with those later that were of the sons of Shem." (288-48) Because of the condition of Uhjltd and Irenan, Ilya was forced to pour water down their throats, hoping to bring them back from the brink of death. After she managed to give them water, she collapsed from her own exhaustion.

Because of the severity of the injuries he had received, Uhjltd underwent a near-death experience. The fall from the kingdom's wall had been traumatic, but the injuries sustained by his near-stoning proved even worse. He was in such physical pain that his consciousness was released from his physical body—an experience that opened him up psychically. According to the readings, this soul ability to transcend the boundaries of his physical body and obtain psychic information would remain with him even when he incarnated thousands of years later as Edgar Cayce:

From this experience, then, does there come that ability for the casting aside of the carnal mind of the physical forces, and there speaks then as the oracles— or to that Throne, or that as builded to which the direction may be sent from those seeking. 294-142

During this near-death experience, Uhjltd also tapped into his past-life memories, witnessed his soul strengths and weaknesses, and gained an awareness of what he was to do with his life. While in this state of consciousness, he also saw images and heard voices reminding him of his mission to bring peace to the desert. At the same time, he beheld images that apparently provided him with a glimpse of the city he was to build. He also underwent some measure of physical healing during his experience.

When Uhjltd finally came back to consciousness, although still in great pain, he managed to pull himself from the cave in search of food. In a short time, he gathered nuts and wild berries and captured a rabbit. He returned to the cave and awakened Ilya. After Ilya and Uhjltd ate, they made a broth from some of the food that Uhjltd had gathered and were able to get some of it into the comatose Irenan to give her a better chance of survival. Meanwhile, the horse that had so faithfully brought them to the abandoned city in the hills and the plains had found plenty of grasses for grazing in the vicinity of the cave and soon completely regained its strength.

During the first few days, Uhjltd instructed Ilya in how to assist him in his own healing, especially using prayer and the laying on of hands. When he was completely well and the days had turned into weeks, the two began exploring their surroundings, finding nuts, berries, and wild grasses that provided them with basic sustenance. Although they suffered many physical hardships, they were alive, and the experience enabled them to call upon their spiritual resources. The influence from this period of their lives as Uhjltd and Ilya remained with them even into the twentieth century: "Though suffering hardships, they learned the lessons of the indwelling of spiritual

forces from within, and the urge in the present from this
we find in the seeking after knowledge of every nature."
(288-10)

When Uhjltd was not scrounging for food or attempting to aid Irenan, he spent much time in meditation and
looking out at the vast expanses of sand and the beauty
of the sky. In the process, his healing and psychic abilities became even more pronounced. He also realized
that he needed supplies and materials for Irenan's healing and their own survival if they were to remain within
the abandoned city. With his faithful horse, Uhjltd made
trips into such places as Egypt, Mesopotamia, and Syria.
He did not return to his native tribe because the tribe
had broken into several factions and many of his own
people had turned against him. The Cayce readings discuss this period of Persian history:

> And in the attempt to then succor this one back
> to life [Irenan], there was the necessity of trips—not
> back to their own people, for the leaders *then* in
> Uhjltd's own guard had turned somewhat against
> him and were attempting to *themselves* become
> leaders, or the rulers of the clans in Iran's lands. In
> these visitations then, to Egypt and to Mesopotamia,
> and to Ibex, and to Syria, there gradually grew up
> about this cave—where this care, or charge, was
> being cared for, that which became a camp. 294-142

In time, Uhjltd and Ilya began to acknowledge their
love for one another. Whenever Uhjltd returned from his
travels, the two were inseparable. As Irenan healed, however, she had a much harder time finding the same peace
of mind in the abandoned city as Ilya and Uhjltd. Although she greatly admired Uhjltd and appeared eager
to learn all that he could teach her, she seemed to resent
the presence of Ilya. Perhaps out of jealousy or perhaps

because she blamed Ilya for their present situation, Irenan often became angry, lashing out at her former pupil. The growing attraction between Uhjltd and Ilya made the situation even more unbearable. It was not unusual for Irenan to be found looking for food for the three on her own, while the other two worked together on something else.

Uhjltd had procured much-needed supplies during his travels. In addition to looking for food, the three also gathered wood for their fires and stitched together blankets and clothing from materials Uhjltd had obtained as well as from the fur and skin of wild creatures they managed to trap. They also spoke of the things that Uhjltd had learned during his near-death experience and spent time in meditation and prayer. Finally, their isolation ended. A caravan happened upon their encampment, and the abandoned city became known once again.

In 1942, during a past-life reading given to a forty-five-year-old man interested in the occult and metaphysics, he was informed that he had been the leader of the first caravan to find the encampment established by Uhjltd, Ilya, and Irenan. In that time, he was interested in the occult and was a soothsayer. He also possessed some talent as a carver of stones. Although it is unclear whether he remained in the city as a permanent resident immediately after his arrival or returned to the city only after completing his original journey, it does appear that Uhjltd and the city became tremendous influences in his life. The experience transformed him from being interested only in self-indulgence to eventually becoming more enlightened and realizing the importance of his influence upon others:

> Before that the entity was in the Persian and Arabian land, in the "city in the hills and the plains," when there was that building of same for those ac-

tivities that were turned into a place of healing, a place of refuge—also as a part of a commercial activity between the east and the west portions of the land.

The entity was that leader of the caravan who first "stumbled," as it were, upon that one who became the teacher in the city then; a soothsayer, a student of the mysteries of the night, the voices—as it were—from the activities in the age or stage of the inter-between.

Then in the name Myrkaw, the entity was a power, a might; but took advantage of those situations—not in that it studied and used the surroundings to self's own indulgence, but in that it used self—through the offices of that entity that builded the city, or under whose direction the city in the hills was builded—to encourage the weak to give outlets for the strong.

There the entity gained and lost and gained. And the abilities in carving stones and setting precious stones became the greater part of the entity's activity, some almost to the undoing—until the enlightening of those tenets of that leader in the "city in the hills." 2761-1

Meanwhile, unknown to the three fugitives, some of Croesus's guards had been looking for them ever since their escape. Among those who hunted for the three was Endessoseu, the guard who had apparently allowed Ilya and Irenan to see Uhjltd in the first place. Somehow, during one of the searches for the prisoners, he became separated from the other guards. As a result, he suffered for many days upon the harsh desert plains and was near death when found by a passing group of travelers who had previously stopped to rest in the city in the hills and the plains. The travelers took Endessoseu back to the city, where he could be healed. After his healing, Endessoseu decided to become a part of the tiny community.

In 1933, a twenty-seven-year-old freight agent and telegrapher was told that he had been one of Croesus's guards—a guard named Endessoseu. His former life had been forever altered after he was brought to the encampment, and the experience still bore a heavy influence on his present life. He was told that he had also been extremely helpful in promoting the city's growth and in communicating its existence to others:

> Before this we find (or in the one before this having an influence in the present experience) the entity was in that land now known as the Arabian, during those periods when there were the establishments of the lands or city where Uhjltd, the leader, the healer, built the city in the hills and the plains.
>
> The entity then was among those of the guard when Uhjltd escaped from the stronghold, and was sent to seek out the one having escaped; suffering for days in the plains and the desert. When found by those that had gained aid through their activity in the hills, the entity was taken in as one badly treated by the elements and cared for; becoming among the first of those to aid in the establishing of the city and the communications with those that passed to and from the eastern to the southern land, or from India to Egypt, from Athens to Egypt.
>
> Then in the name Endessoseu, in the experience as a whole, the entity developed; developed through the activities and through the influences that were brought to bear on the entity, in keeping both the commands when under the soldiery of the Persian peoples and the mental commands and experiences of the leader in the plain; aiding throughout the whole experience in bringing aid to the sick and

afflicted. Also the entity aided in teaching much to those of the varied lands.

Hence the abilities in the present as to the understandings; so that the entity is able to bring about an understanding between those where differences of any nature have existed in the minds or experiences of others.

Also there are the abilities in the fields of activity that will bring experiences to others that will enable them to help themselves. 416-1

When the three were no longer isolated and the time came for another trip into Egypt, Ilya and Uhjltd decided to make the journey together, leaving Irenan with the newcomers who now also called the city their home. The couple's love had blossomed, and they could no longer ignore their physical desire for one another. On the evening before their journey, they bathed themselves in the cool waters of one of the underground springs and reclined on a bed of skins:

. . . and there watch the sun's slow sinking over the desert sands. And in this fading hour they first find the answer of body to body in the soul's awakening, as they melt into one; giving then an offering to the world, who, in the form and in the stature of the great leader, gave the first philosophy of life and love to the world [Zend?], coming from this union. 288-6

According to the Cayce readings, that night as they lay together as one, Ilya conceived a son. From that day on, Uhjltd and Ilya lived together as husband and wife.

In time, the tiny city came to be called Is-Shlan-doen. It served as an ideal stopping place for merchants and wearied travelers journeying between other cities. The rolling hillsides soon were spotted with tents so those who stopped could refresh and rejuvenate themselves before continuing their journeys. On occasion, people who had been cast out from their homelands or who were fleeing from one kind of oppression or another decided to stay, making the small encampment their home. Livestock sometimes arrived with travelers, so that a few sheep, cattle, and horses also became a part of the area. In order to supplement the berries and nuts that grew in the encampment, various crops and trees were planted, and water from the underground springs was diverted into irrigation systems. It soon became evident that the warm climate and the availability of water made the area ideal for growing a variety of produce.

Uhjltd began to teach those who lived in the community as well as anyone who visited the tiny settlement. When asked what Uhjltd taught the people, Cayce replied, "that which brought about in that day the better understanding of the relationships of man to man, and man to his Maker." (294-144) Uhjltd encouraged the residents to put away their petty feelings, their distrust, and their fears of others. All who listened were told that, rather than might making right, "the power of love makes right." (1567-2) He inspired his listeners to become aware of their relationships with and their responsibility toward one another. He encouraged people to become more in touch with their spiritual source, and he also began teaching a variety of healing techniques that he had learned in his travels.

Because of the city's location, its emphasis on peace, Uhjltd's teachings, and the fact that every person was welcome, regardless of class, the news spread far and wide that the city of Is-Shlan-doen had something special to offer. Rumors also grew that this man Uhjltd was much more than simply a mortal man:

There were the associations with varied groups, varied members of the groups that were as natives as well as the Persians, and those who made treks from various portions of the country. The center gradually began to be known as a place not only for refuge, for those of the various groups through the land, but as a place of teaching. 288-48

In the days then that followed, with this gradual building up from those that had been first as outcasts from their own kind, in the various spheres of experience, the entity builded a great city—or *rather* a great *field* of tents! and the teachings that were given by the emissaries who came in from many lands, when there were the establishing of greater associations. For the *power* of the leader then went out, gradually, by the efforts of those emissaries, as made for a power to be reckoned with among the nations. For there was rather that which bore upon the people, that this man was of heaven, rather than of earth. 294-142

In addition to various outcasts, merchants, and travelers, a number of advisors and emissaries from other lands began to journey to the city to witness for themselves what was occurring within the desert hills and plains. What they learned of value they took with them back to their own cities and countries.

During this early period in the city's new history, the infighting within the remnants of Uhjltd's former tribe continued. Uhjltd's father, Eujueltd, had joined forces with Oujida in an attempt to overpower a rival claim to leadership. The ongoing hostilities within the tribe had prompted Slumdki to return to Egypt. Those who remained with the original settlement were still subject to invasions by various tribes in both Persia and Lydia. The

people were so divided and they experienced such persecution and ongoing conflicts that finally the old tribe
was broken apart. With the demise of Ra and Zu, a number of the people became wanderers. Some joined rival
tribes, while others followed the example of Slumdki and
sought exile in Egypt. However, there were a few who had
heard of the activities in the hills and the plains, and they
sought refuge in Uhjltd's city.

In August 1940, Edgar Cayce advised a fifty-eight-year-
old restaurant owner that he had been among the wanderers of Ra and Zu who had sought out his former
leader, hoping to find a new life in the revived city. What
he found in Is-Shlan-doen also gave him a way to bring
help to others:

> The entity then was among those peoples to
> which Uhjltd belonged. Hence with the uprisings
> that came about, with the banishment or loss of
> Uhjltd as a tribesman, the entity sought out those
> activities of Uhjltd, by the individual search.
>
> Hence we find the entity oft latently desiring to
> go alone; and yet always depending upon and in-
> fluenced by others. These are well when used aright.
> These may become stumbling-stones when the ide-
> als and purposes are lost in the idiosyncrasies or
> mere ideas of others.
>
> The name then was Esdraexon. In the experience
> the entity gained throughout; for with the seeking
> out of the leader and teacher, and the activities
> which brought about the great service to others, the
> entity became as a living poem in the service to oth-
> ers; in making song, in making psalms, in making
> rime of the happenings of others from other lands,
> as well as those who joined with that group there-
> about.
>
> Thus we find that great latent and manifested

force in the abilities for the entity to apply same in the experience of any form in the daily life.

In that period the entity acted as an interpreter, as an aid to many who came from other lands. 2337-1

In addition to people from the two tribes who sought out Uhjltd, citizens of Croesus's kingdom gradually began to come to the city as well. Rumors of Uhjltd's spiritual nature seemed far removed from the anger, tyranny, and control of King Croesus. The Cayce readings suggest that even some of those who had once hated Uhjltd and his people for the tribe's attack on Croesus's city and the temple school eventually looked on Is-Shlan-doen in friendship. One of the most notable examples is the case of a woman named Gracia, who had apparently been one of the teachers of the maidens in the school. For a long while after the attack, the readings said, she held a grudge against Uhjltd. She later journeyed to the city, however, and became involved in spiritual training for the city's young women:

> The entity then, in the name Gracia, came to be what would today be called the Mother Superior to the schools as they were gathered for the young ladies or girls of the city builded in that place. The entity in the latter portion of the experience became a help and aid to those that led in the upbuilding for the peoples of many nations.
>
> Hence languages, or the activities of peoples in various walks of life, even in the present—as through the experiences in the sojourns in various planes— make for an understanding to the entity in the present. 403-1

Another subject of Croesus came to Is-Shlan-doen during the city's early development. Skilled in communication, she served as an interpreter for the people who found their way to the encampment. She also became a part of the healing activities that Uhjltd was establishing:

> Before that the entity was in the Persian and Arabian land, when those activities of the teacher brought healing to many of the Persians.
>
> For, the entity was among those of the household of the king, Croesus, who had been in reign over that land. With the establishing of the "city in the hills and the plains," the entity sought out those activities, as they became known throughout the many lands, as that center developed.
>
> There the entity aided in the healing activities, and in the preparing of the messages for the varied groups from the Indian, Egyptian and other lands. For, this became as a center through which the various caravans traveled. Thus the entity became what today would be called a linguist, but an interpreter of messages for various groups . . .
>
> The name then was Cherreu. 3003-1

As the small encampment grew, it became obvious that the city needed to prepare itself for an increasing population. With that in mind, all who arrived found plenty of work with which to occupy their time. Places around the surrounding hillsides needed to be cleared for the raising of tents. The irrigation system was expanded, as were the fields of crops. Due to the periodic cycles of the growing season as well as the fluctuation of both the permanent and transitory population, excavations were made for underground storehouses for food, and warehouses were built for supplies.

Is-Shlan-doen's reputation as a way station and a place of rest for travelers from both east and west spread across the region. With the influx of caravans and people from many cultures and backgrounds, trade and commerce within the city's borders became inevitable, as did the need for interpreters and various media of exchange.

Some also saw the city as a place for travelers passing through to discard servants who had outlived their usefulness or to leave behind those who were on the verge of death from illness or old age. Edgar Cayce even informed a thirty-nine-year-old woman that, in a previous life, she was born in the city during that period, apparently to passing travelers, and was immediately abandoned and left behind: "In the 'city in the hills and the plains' we find the entity was among the first of those born in that city, that was established by the teacher Uhjltd there; the entity being among those peoples who were left or deserted by the travelers through the land." (2073-2) It became apparent that Uhjltd's knowledge of healing needed to be disseminated to the people. In time, a structure was built—a hospital of its day—where people could find healing, recuperation, or recovery of one kind or another. *Healing Center*

The activity that threatened King Croesus II the most, however, was not that Is-Shlan-doen provided a place of healing or that Uhjltd provided spiritual knowledge to those who would listen. Instead, it was that the city in the hills and the plains had begun to offer a place of trade and commerce beyond the king's borders and the reach of his tax collectors.

4

From Hillside Encampment
to Desert Metropolis

In large measure, word of the existence of Is-Shlan-doen was carried across the desert in the caravans of merchants and tradesmen. The city championed itself as a place where the universality of the one God was made a practical experience in people's relationships with one another. It was no secret that Uhjltd hoped his message of peace and humanity's interdependence would be carried far beyond the desert. As visitors passed through the ever-growing encampment, rumors of the city spread throughout much of the known world. When some heard the tales, they scoffed that such a thing was only a fable, but many more detoured from their normal trade routes in order to see the city first-hand.

444 — 11/12/00

In 1944, a sixty-one-year-old U.S. Navy food inspector received a reading and was told that he had been among the traveling merchants to the city. At that time, he specialized in a variety of goods that he traded along his expansive route:

> Before that we find the entity was in the Persian land, among those who carried the goods from one portion of the land to another, or a caravan maker, dealing in the linens of Egypt, the pearls of Persia, in the opal, the firestone, the lapis lazuli in Indo-China, yea the diamonds and rubies of some of the cities of gold. These find an attraction for the entity in the experience in the present. Be not rather as a hoarder but use such, then, of the knowledge of such, in the study as to the helpful force in the experience of thy fellow man.
>
> The name then was Taian. 5294-1

In the beginning, the encampment was a stopping point for caravans because of its ideal location in the middle of the desert hills and plains. The city provided a safe haven where one might rest from the threat of desert bandits or where travelers could obtain food and water before continuing their journeys. Eventually, the variety of people from different cultures using Is-Shlan-doen as a way station to traverse the desert only heightened its popularity because of the potential for exchanging ideas around campfires and merchants' tables. During the early years, the city was known primarily as a place of refuge and rest and, secondly, as a place of learning.

Travelers learned from one another, exchanging information about possible trade routes or discussing problems that had occurred on previous journeys. The likelihood of potential problems with nomadic warriors or traveling thieves was also a subject of discussion.

Many of the travelers had the opportunity to speak with Uhjltd or were present as he taught around a campfire. Much that he had to offer seemed to inspire his listeners and take hold as the tenets of a great truth communicated with simplicity. In addition to the oneness of God and the interconnectedness of the Creator's human children, those tenets included the necessity of applying seemingly little things, such as gentleness, patience, and the giving of a smile; the importance of truth; and the desirability of refraining from verbal or armed warfare. The information grew popular because of its availability to all, regardless of background, and the fact that no special training or secret initiation was required of the seeker.

A twenty-seven-year-old photographer was told in a reading that he had been involved in the city "when there first began the buildings in that land of those that gathered about the teacher Uhjltd on the hill and the plain land." Arriving as a Tibetan lama with different beliefs, he soon decided to stay and take part in a spiritual work that emphasized the equality of all:

> During the experience the entity gained; for making practical application by the teacher in the plain brought much that had been a mystery to the entity—as Zeulan—to the understanding that the *spirit* maketh the most lowly alive, and the soul of same may develop into a thing of beauty, whether in the high, the low or the intermediate castes; for these are ever in the presence of those that look on material things. But to all is given that ability to use what they have for the service of the Creative Influence in the experience of all.
>
> The entity gained in the experience, and in the present the Vedas or those things that pertain to the mysteries of old arise much from that experience.

Yet, if the entity makes the tenets of the day as practical in the dealings with the individuals whom the
entity contacts day by day, the entity may gain even
as in that sojourn. 315-4

[handwritten margin note: its the little things in each interaction]

In time, men who made the city in the hills and the
plains their home became considerably different from
men of other cities and tribes. In part, that difference
was in affirming the equality of women. Uhjltd's guidance also taught that all people should attempt to experience for themselves oneness with the Creator and the
all-abiding presence of Spirit as active and practical in
their everyday lives. Uhjltd tried to get people in touch
with the goodness that often was dormant within them.
He hoped to encourage them to align their physical bodies with their spiritual Source. For that reason, meditation and prayer became regular components of everyday
life. There was even a periodic call to worship which, according to the Cayce readings, later was adopted by
members of the Islamic faith:

Before that we find the entity was in that land
now known as the Persian, during those experiences when there was the tented city in the hills and
plains.

The entity was among those of the household of
the leader in that experience, bringing through
those relationships the closer relations with those
from the varied activities of those that had joined
themselves for the various purposes of understandings in that experience; in the name then Joyel.

The entity gained much, for the music that became a portion of the call that has come down to
the Moslems, the East Indians, the call to worship,
was begun by the entity in that experience; which
has made for that in the hearts and minds of many

why "call to prayer"

as a means, a manner of giving expression materi-
ally to the promptings from within. 324-5

The city acted as a type of leavening for people
throughout the region. Uhjltd championed peace, and
peace became established in much of the area. His goal
was to form an allied relationship with all others as a
natural consequence of people recognizing their mutual
interdependence. For a time, it even appeared that his
goal had been realized. One concept he taught was that
a major purpose of life is for people to recognize their
obligation to others, lending aid and service in the process. As more people began to follow this concept, the
work of healing was expanded. The city that had first
been known as a place of rest and then as a place of
learning soon became championed as a place of healing.

One of the reasons that Edgar Cayce so frequently referred to the activities in ancient Persia as having a
strong bearing on his own work in the twentieth century
was because of this emphasis on healing. Just as Cayce
had spent much of his life focusing on the importance of
health and the body-mind-soul connection, the city of
Is-Shlan-doen provided people with much more than
spiritual direction. Certainly, all who arrived within the
city's borders soon heard Uhjltd's spiritual principles.
For example, in 1935, Cayce told a forty-nine-year-old
woman that any who came for healing were taught, "As
ye do it to thy brethren, as ye show forth the purpose for
which ye entered, ye are healed." (1037-1) On another
occasion, a forty-seven-year-old man was informed of
his own involvement in the city and of the tenets that
became a part of his experience:

*Do Purpose
Be Healed*

> The entity then was among the Persians who
> came into the "city in the hills and the plains," aid-
> ing that leader, that teacher there to make practical

in the experiences of those that came as wanderers or as seekers the proclaiming of the perfect day of those that sought for healing in body, in mind, and in the understanding of those simple truths that have ever been, will ever be, the way that binds the hearts and minds of men to their relationship to the Creative Forces, "As ye do it unto the least of thy brethren," the manner in which ye mete thine activities of love, of hope, of patience, of way of living to thy fellowman, ye do it unto thy God! *As you Treat Others you Treat God*

For as thy brother, as thy fellowman is as thyself a representative, a portion of that Love, that Hope, that *Soul* that is the kinship to the Father-God, so as ye treat thy fellowman ye do it unto thy Maker. 1151-1

Healing Modalities:

The spiritual counsel was supplemented, however, by the use of every imaginable type of healing in the city's hospital. In addition to using the skills of the physicians and nurses of the day, the hospital also employed counselors, physical therapists, musicians, color therapists, and people trained in hydrotherapy, the laying on of hands, prayer, gems and stones, diet and exercise, and the application of various ointments, topical remedies, and lotions. The city also eventually championed the necessity of caring for the elderly, the terminally ill, the destitute, and the infirm. In fact, the readings told one person who had been a nurse in her past life in Persia that the care, companionship, and healing methods available to patients "went much beyond mere nursing." (2862-1) In time, the hospital even offered vocational guidance. Another important principle was an emphasis on sanitation and personal cleanliness. The necessity of remaining close to nature and the elements of the earth also became important principles of the city's healing ministry.

A sixty-three-year-old chiropractor was informed that his present-day talent with healing was traceable to this period in ancient Persia. In that experience, he became adept at using hot and cold hydrotherapy in conjunction with physical adjustments, providing release from the pain caused by muscular or skeletal problems. He was also particularly skilled at relieving the discomfort associated with colds and congestion. Cayce said that the chiropractor retained a thorough understanding of the physical body and encouraged him to continue his work in the present, focusing especially on orthopedics or physiotherapy. (3042-1)

In another instance, a twenty-year-old secretary was told that she had been associated with the healing work in Is-Shlan-doen. Her present-day ability to become quiet and centered, listening to her own spiritual nature or simply enjoying the beauty of the stars or her surroundings, was connected to her Persian incarnation. There, she had been a musician, using her talent in the healing arts as a method of soothing people and quieting their fears. She was told that she retained those same musical abilities within herself and that—because of that past-life experience—she could also discover a personal aptitude for helping others through the use of movement and dance (2700-1).

In 1937, a forty-seven-year-old housewife was told that her ability to work with healing through prayer and the laying on of hands—especially with members of her own family—had been acquired in ancient Persia:

> The entity was among the natives that came with the first of the caravans that made for those activities where it became a place of healing.
>
> The entity became a healer . . .
>
> And the entity may be—if it will apply itself—a *healer* to others, even by the laying on of hands.

(For the vibrations are high, and these are of the healing nature to those especially who are troubled with those things that have raised the emotions to detrimental influences to the whole of the assimilation; the assimilating system, to the nervous system, to the heart's activity, to the influences where destruction of self is at times felt necessary.)

(The entity may soothe, the entity may cause all such to become quiet.)

For the entity gained through that experience much that if applied in the present may become very, very worth while; not only for the assurance that is always sought in self but for the help, the hope it may bring to others.

For after all, the whole duty of man in any experience is to show forth the love the Father has shown, in the manner and in the way as to bring hope to those that—from the material things—have lost sight of the promises to the children of men. 1469-1

The city's focus on the healing arts proved to be a major attraction for people from every walk of life, culture, and level of society. From all over the continent they came into the city for personal healing or to become a part of the hospital and of the healing ministry that was bustling with activities. Stories of the amazing healings that took place—like stories about Uhjltd's teaching—spread with the passage of countless travelers. Cayce told a sixty-three-year-old widow that she had been a princess from another country at the time and had abandoned her heritage to come to the city and to learn to serve as a nurse. The woman was advised that, for her work, she had "advanced in spirit, in mind, and in its united effort for the common good of all." (3006-1)

On a number of occasions, those who were told by Cayce in the present that they had once been a part of the healing work in Is-Shlan-doen were also advised that they still retained those abilities at a soul level. To be sure, all were not presently employed in the health care fields nor were they all told to explore the same line of work in the present. Nonetheless, their talents as caregivers could still be expressed in a variety of ways. For example, in 1943, a thirty-five-year-old housewife was told:

> The entity was among those who contributed much to the welfare of those who sought help from the teacher.
>
> Thus the entity is one who in a visit to a sick room may make the day all the brighter, but not as a nurse, rather as one who might talk with those that are ill. For it can laugh with those who laugh and weep with those who mourn.
>
> Keep close to this in all of thy activities. For here ye may contribute often that which will be the helpful force to those who are seeking—seeking—that which seems to be so far away.
>
> Then in the name Edeth, the entity gained. In the present there are the abilities to contribute to welfare work, to be an aid in visiting those who are sick or shut-in, and in not distributing tracts but in telling that which ye have heard, and telling others that they may experience it themselves. And be kind to children. 3374-1

As news of the existence of Is-Shlan-doen spread across the continent, the city required better methods of organization to deal with the ever-growing number of visitors. The days of simply arriving at the tiny encampment and having occasion to speak with Uhjltd or converse with fellow travelers around a campfire were no longer possible when the few visitors became hundreds or thousands instead. Eventually, it became necessary for the city to hire gatekeepers, who met all merchants, travelers, and visitors at the entrance to the city and interviewed them to determine their needs. Those who came to the city to rest and refresh themselves before continuing their journeys were directed to one portion of the city. Merchants who came to exchange goods or barter were sent to the central marketplace. Any who required healing were guided toward the city's hospital. Those who had simply traveled to hear the teachings of Uhjltd were told when he would next speak and what they might do to occupy their time in the interim.

It is important to point out that, in spite of Uhjltd's teachings and the city's goal of becoming a model for cooperation and the application of spiritual principles in the earth, everything was not perfect in Is-Shlandoen. A number of people used the city's existence as a means to satisfy their personal interests or to acquire material wealth. One example pointed out by the Cayce readings was that, as the number of visitors continued to grow and the need for multiple gatekeepers expanded, a few turned to accepting bribes in return for addressing travelers' needs more speedily. In 1935, Edgar Cayce told a thirty-seven-year-old lawyer that he had been one of the gatekeepers who had accepted bribes and that, although he had gained because of his understanding of people from many cultures, he had eventually lost in soul growth because of his actions:

> The entity then was—what now would be called—the keeper of the gate in those experiences; or the one that would separate those that were of the various climes or those that were dis-eased and those that were diseased, that there might be the better activities with the accomplishments to be had or to be received through the leader during those experiences.

Then the entity came close in associations with the ruler of the city, but more in the capacity of questioning with and understanding those of different lands and other climes, other religions and other anticipations or religious activities, that came desiring and seeking reliefs from whatever sources they came.

In a portion of the experience the entity gained, and in a portion there were the self-indulgences and the self-aggrandizements; for the entity turned toward that attitude that there should be tribute paid to self—or that there should be the returns for making the quicker associations or getting in contact with those things necessary for the relief. This brought to the entity destructive influences. 914-1

In addition to his magnetism and wisdom, part of Uhjltd's popularity was due to his own healing and psychic abilities, both of which had been enhanced by his near-death experience. The readings suggest that Uhjltd taught people how they could begin to heal others through the laying on of hands. His psychic ability was also advantageous in enabling him to discern those who might be best able to assist in administering the needs of the city. Uhjltd was not the only one known for his use of intuition within the city's borders, however. Apparently, the city also employed several people skilled in the use of their psychic gifts. Those abilities helped them ascertain the talents, needs, and appropriate occupation for travelers coming into the city. For example, a thirty-eight-year-old woman learned that she had been one of the city's "soothsayers," possessing the ability to read the signs of the sand, the sun, the moon, and the stars in order to learn about all those who came to settle in Is-Shlan-doen (2408-1). Another woman was told that she joined the city while it served as a commercial center as well as a place for instruction in the mental and spiritual aspects of human relationships. She was informed that she was among the East Indian people who settled in the city and that she served as "a soothsayer" and "a mystic" (2441-2).

Uhjltd's popularity and the many demands on his time all required a great deal of help from others in order for him to fulfill his own duties and keep track of the activities within and needs of the city. Surprisingly, perhaps, one of his greatest helpers came in the form of a twelve-year-old boy named Esdena, who grew to become one of Uhjltd's most trusted advisors.

Esdena was actually a cousin, the son of Uhjltd's father's brother. He had stayed with what remained of the tribes of Ra and Zu even after Oujida had moved the settlement into Egypt. With the final dissolution of the tribe, Esdena became one of those who wandered, eventually finding his way to the city in the hills and the plains. Sometime during the youth's harsh journey, the boy contracted malaria. Esdena was healed by Uhjltd personally and soon joined Uhjltd and Ilya as a member of their household. As Esdena grew older, several people—perhaps out of jealousy—tried to come between him and his influence on Uhjltd. But the young man's innate wisdom and his ability to gather information about the various immigrants to the city proved extremely worthwhile, and his influence with Uhjltd continued.

The readings suggest that, because of Esdena's fact-finding in the form of written diaries, others were able to deduce the nearly limitless possibilities for trade and commerce that existed within the city. Apparently, many of those who journeyed to Is-Shlan-doen brought fruits, vegetables, and merchandise with them to offer in exchange for healing. This fact, in addition to the presence of so many merchants and caravans using the city as a way station, suggested that the possibilities for trade and commerce within the city were not yet fully realized.

During the course of a follow-up life reading for the thirty-four-year-old attorney who was told that he had been Esdena, Cayce described his activities and talents:

The entity showed its greater aptitude in gathering data from the various groups that came, for the one purpose or another, to that Center (as we will call it). For the varied groups, as of the period, brought the fruits of their individual lands or vicinities as in exchange for that given out in the healings or the teachings or the counsel, the advice, the awakening of the possibilities in that which would arise in the experience of individuals and groups. For the cooperative forces were those things that made for the greater interest to Esdena, as he began the compilations of what might be well termed in the present a diary of happenings in and about that city; and particularly as pertaining to the character of advice and counsel that was given by Uhjltd, in the manners especially of the various groups, depending upon the elements in the soil, the air, the sun, the water. For what would become the sustaining forces for the bodies, first; and for the minds by the occupations in the creative forces of a universal activity among the individuals that so applied themselves . . .

The entity then, Esdena, began this rather as that of advice from the leader Uhjltd, who aided in recalling the varied incidents and classifying the activities as to the manners in which the various groups from the various lands were included. Those that bore the vine, the fig tree, corn, the fruits of the fields, the fruits of the herds, and those as applied in the experience of individuals; including, to be sure, those adornments of body, those spices of preservation, those that are called condiments in foods, cosmetics in adornment, and money in exchange. These all were included in those activities, you see, that were set for the various groups; that later—under the supervision of others—made for the opening of the place of exchange between the varied lands that gradually became represented by various groups and individuals, as there began the correlations of what had been gathered by the entity.

So the entity rose gradually in authority or power, or as to those things wherein there might be the more reliance put in what was given as to the activities of those in the varied lands, as well as their own. This made for that which was injected in that given respecting the entity, that he became the "right hand man" of the leader Uhjltd. 826-4

When it became clear that the city was fast becoming as much a center for commerce as for healing, the need to organize the land and its inhabitants into a proper metropolis also became apparent. Keeping all of the various purposes of Is-Shlan-doen in mind, city leaders laid out a new plan, one that considered the needs of the populace as well as those of the countless visitors who came for various purposes. The reorganization also took into account necessities such as food, water, and the proper disposal of garbage and human waste. The ability to defend the city against invaders, as well as from possible uprisings among the transient nomads and merchants, was an important consideration as well. The numerous caves throughout the city were put to good use, either for housing or for storage. During this same period, many of the tent structures were replaced with more permanent buildings of stone and wood.

As the city's fame and prosperity grew, so, too, did the

number of people who found themselves in opposition to what was occurring in Is-Shlan-doen, either because it threatened their own treasuries or because of jealousy. Some of the warring nomads felt that might and power remained superior to any of the tenets that Uhjltd hoped to establish in the city. The rumors of wealth trading hands within the borders of this city of peace seemed all too tempting to some. But perhaps the greatest threat was Croesus II. His own treasury had begun to dwindle as more and more commercial activities occurred within Is-Shlan-doen. Finally, he decided to act.

5

Life in the City

Croesus II grew increasingly more threatened by the existence of Is-Shlan-doen. In addition to desert oasis and healing locale, the city was gradually becoming the most prominent and thriving center for trade and commerce. Far too many merchants now bypassed the king's territories in favor of the city in the hills and the plains, angering not only the king but some of the noble families as well. With the arrival of caravans from all over the continent, the encampment had grown into an enormous metropolis. In response to the persistent activity, the city had been forced to set up mediums of exchange with other nations and was in frequent communication with an ever-growing number of cultures and lands to the north and the south, in the Far East, in Egypt, and among the people bordering the Great Sea.

After the defection of Endessoseu and others, an increasing number of Croesus's subjects found themselves attracted to Uhjltd's city, making the threat even worse. According to the readings, even Croesus's aunt became interested in the activities occurring in Is-Shlan-doen. The twentieth-century woman who was told that, in a previous life, she had been the king's aunt was informed that she was drawn to the city because of one of Uhjltd's tenets: that each and every soul has a connection to the Creator. She also came to realize that an essential purpose of life was to recognize that relationship and what it truly means about each soul's ultimate connection to all other souls (1007-3). With the threat of competing commerce, the defection of some of his own people, and the influence Is-Shlan-doen was having far beyond its borders, Croesus finally had had enough.

Oneness

The Cayce readings do not state when Croesus launched his first attack. What is clear is that Uhjltd had already assembled a group of warriors as an extremely capable line of defense. Perhaps surprisingly, Croesus and his forces were quickly defeated by the same city that extolled the virtues of peace. Extremely stubborn, Croesus regrouped his troops and attacked a second time. Again, he was sorely defeated. When it became clear that the city was capable of defending itself, the plan for a direct assault was set aside for a period. Instead, rather than risking another defeat, the king's army and some of the nomadic tribes decided that a better course of action might be to attack the caravans on their journey to Is-Shlan-doen. For that reason, travelers and merchants suddenly needed more protection from mercenary patrols and desert bandits than they had previously. As a result, Uhjltd put in place soldiers who guided travelers and caravans through the desert, providing safe passage along trade routes and among scattered desert springs and places of refuge. Croesus refused to change his mind about such attacks, however, and, for a long while, he

War/Peace

continued to sponsor occasional raids on traveling merchants.

In addition to angering Croesus and some of the noble families, Is-Shlan-doen's ongoing success proved to be a point of contention for a number of others: those who refused to accept what Uhjltd was trying to accomplish and instead did everything they could to undermine it. For that reason, Uhjltd used his army to deflect the occasional threat that arose from one of the surrounding tribes. There were also other challenges beyond those of military entanglements. As a case in point, Edgar Cayce informed a thirty-seven-year-old professor with an innate talent for business that he had been among Uhjltd's detractors. At the time, he loved business and commerce and felt that the city's tenets threatened his ability to acquire personal wealth. Cayce advised him that one of the lessons he could still learn in the present was that brotherly love and business expertise did not need to exist as contrary ideas:

> The entity was among the Persians who were gradually taken over in part, yet the entity *never* was among those who became submissive to, or who joined in the activities in the "city in the hills and the plains," but was one who despised (as would be termed in present terminology) those activities which wrought such an influence during that experience. For, the entity was of that *cult* as would be termed of the capitalistic nature today; hence might made right (in its final analysis).
>
> As a business executive, influences arise in the present from that experience that make the abilities good in the entity—*for* business. For the expansions—let love rule; and we may find that these *can* and may be worked together. 2381-1

Once the dangers from Croesus and the rival nomadic tribes lessened to some extent, Uhjltd was able to return to focusing on the needs of his own family. By this time, Ilya had given birth to a son, and they had named the child Zend. Because of his own intuitive abilities, Uhjltd knew from the very beginning that his son was destined to become a great spiritual leader. For that reason, Uhjltd began teaching Zend, even as an infant, the spiritual truths and knowledge he had acquired. Ilya proved a tremendous influence on her son, as well. Her own noble upbringing and training, coupled with the insights she had acquired from working with her husband, proved invaluable at providing the child with—what might be termed in the present—a well-rounded education.

As the city's reputation grew, a number of Uhjltd's family members who had been with him in the previous tribal settlement found their way into the city. Even Uhjltd's father, Eujueltd, came to the city and reconciled with his eldest son. Although broken in body and spirit because of the harsh years upon the desert, Eujueltd remembered the faith of his youth and eventually became one of the most gifted healers in the city. He seemed to have a natural talent for the practice of laying on of hands and quickly became invaluable in the activities in the city's hospital. Uhjltd's mother, Slumdki, also journeyed to Is-Shlan-doen, becoming, as well, an integral part of life in the city as well.

In 1930, Cayce informed the fifty-year-old widow who had been Slumdki that, from her Persian incarnation, she still retained the ability to direct and control individuals and groups. Apparently, in the city of the hills and the plains, she became quite active in city affairs and eventually was elevated to the status of benevolent queen:

In the one before this we find in that land known

now as the Persian. The entity then among those peoples of the nomads, and the mother to the ruler who *conquered* the Persian peoples; giving much to the ruler, Uhjltd, in that period, through counsel, advice, and coming as an aid *to* those peoples that were subdued, and teaching much *in* the land—in ensample; that, though there were condemnations, and there were the misunderstandings in the purpose of the raids, or the conquering of the peoples, the entity held *little* against the peoples, and became the ruler, the Queen, of that divided land. In the name Slumdki. In the present experience, those of the psychic forces as come as impressions in meditation. Those in abilities of business, of being able to direct and to control groups, come from the innate experience of the entity. Able, in and through that experience, to control the servant as well as the ruler. 2708-1

In addition to his parents, some of Uhjltd's siblings found their way into the city. According to the readings, Uhjltd's youngest sister, Celca, arrived in Is-Shlan-doen and eventually became a linguist, assisting travelers from various locations. She also joined with those who served as entertainers, providing amusement and diversion to the populace and the city's visitors. Uhjltd's younger brother, Uhjenda, proved as skillful with the laying on of hands as his father. The young man also inherited some of his older brother's intuitive abilities, a skill he used to ascertain the spiritual, mental, and physical needs of those who came for healing. Another of Uhjltd's brothers, Elhasen, was apparently proficient at politics and mediation. With the establishment of Is-Shlan-doen as a center for trade, he eventually rose to the position of what might be called mayor.

Ilya's former instructress, Irenan, still remained in the

city. However, the additional demands Uhjltd now had on his time, plus the presence of more family members, his wife, and a child, all added to Irenan's jealousy. Perhaps she remained in the city because she hoped things would change or that she might find occasion to at least spend more time with the man she had come to revere, but she was not happy. In addition to Uhjltd's family, there was also the ever-present Esdena and any number of advisors and tradesmen who vied for an audience with the leader. As a result, Irenan isolated herself and was not an active part of the city's tremendous growth.

From the central cave that Ilya and Uhjltd still used as their home, Is-Shlan-doen expanded in every direction. The expansion resulted in the birth of a model city with comprehensive irrigation and waste-removal systems. The city's output in livestock, agriculture, and produce was greater than that of any society since Egypt. Much of the area was found to be rich in various minerals and precious gems, all adding to the city's commerce and wealth. A number of cultural and social improvements also enhanced Is-Shlan-doen's image as the perfect city. By this time, the city in the hills and the plains provided many with physical healing, mental counsel, and spiritual awakening.

Over the years that Edgar Cayce gave readings, the past-life stories of numerous people provided insights into life in this ancient metropolis as well as the activities with which the reading recipients were involved. In addition to the soldiers and warriors who protected travelers and citizens, the city had a sheriff who also doubled as one of the people in charge of entertainment. During a life reading, a forty-two-year-old drug salesman learned that he had been that sheriff:

> The entity was among those set in charge of the
> entertainment, or to make the people feel "at

home," or to protect the city from those who were in the various caravans who were not of the same mind as the peoples in the "city in the hills."

Hence the entity was what today would be termed the sheriff or policeman of that place at that time; thus in another direction seeking the cooperative measures between various types of people, various groups and various activities.

Thus in the present, we find the entity a very good mixer with peoples.

The name then was Hassar. 5154-1

There was a legal system in the city that provided for the tempering of justice with mercy. Laws were enacted to enforce the city's guidelines for peace and cooperation, as well as those that dealt with trade and commerce. In a reading given to an eight-year-old boy, the parents learned that their son had served the city as a counselor and judge. In that capacity, he worked with both social and commercial concerns. He also found occasion to interpret the laws for those who frequented the city from different lands (305-3).

A forty-two-year-old housewife and artist was told that her skills with cooking could be traced back to a Persian lifetime when she had excelled at both baking and weaving. During that experience, she frequently found occasion to use ovens out in the open, apparently cooking for large numbers of people. At the same time, because of the number of people from many cultures and backgrounds who came into the city, she became talented at working with all kinds of garments and apparel. In the present, she was encouraged to continue using her culinary and artistic skills, particularly directing her art into painting and tapestry (718-2).

A 1930s entertainer and singer learned that her talent with song and dance had also been cultivated in Is-

Shlan-doen: "the entity became one that gave much to the peoples in the way of expressing to them, in song *and* dance, the efforts *of* the peoples in the home land, of trying or attempting to bring joy, or opening *of* the life to the efforts, or that expressed in nature." (2134-1) Because of her talents in that past life, she became a favorite of many in her audiences. Although she gained in that lifetime for her ability to inspire others, she eventually lost as well for using her influence for her <u>own selfish</u> <u>motives</u>.

Stops Soul Advancement

The city's entertainment was not limited to song and dance. Another person receiving a reading had apparently been employed as some kind of writer and drawer of caricatures. Her work portrayed all phases of life in the city, from healing and spirituality to the pursuit of love and even commercial success. In addition to her artistic talents, she eventually became a teacher, often exploring the activities, manners, and customs of the various groups who inhabited Is-Shlan-doen (2329-1).

In time, the dramatic arts became an important focal point for many in the city. As the regular demands of life were met, people found time for culture and diversion. One woman learned that her work with drama and elocution and her efforts at helping others appreciate the beauty of the human form were later expanded and adopted by the Greeks. A skilled instructor, she was encouraged to continue her work with others in the present and to focus some of her abilities on the interpretation of art and drama or as a critic in either area (1167-2).

Repeatedly, those who received life readings from Edgar Cayce and who were told that they had been a part of the Persian period were informed that the experience still influenced their life in the present. In 1938, a fifty-seven-year-old librarian learned that her love of Persia was traceable to an incarnation at the time of Uhjltd:

Only when the entity then, as Saujued, assisted in the ministering to those through the experiences in the "city in the hills and the plains" were there the well-established teachings among those of the many lands, as to the needs for and the directing of those tenets and teachings through those experiences.

For the entity gained throughout, by the service to others.

In the present we find from same that those things of the nature pertaining to Persian colors, Persian activities, Persian rugs, Persian things that give expression to the intermingling of all the vibrations, become a part of the experience of the entity innately and manifestedly.

Also there are the abilities in the present, from that sojourn, to analyze individuals in their relationships to groups whom they may serve; whether it be teachers, ministers, lawyers, doctors or what— that are *supposed* as groups to serve the whole and not themselves! 1648-1

In another case history, the life reading for a fifty-year-old clerk stated that he had once been an important merchant from Baghdad. During that incarnation, he specialized in selling sweet incense and found a ready market in the land of the Egyptians, where they used the incense not only for the preservation of the dead, but also as a part of everyday life in the temples and homes. Coming under Uhjltd's influence, the merchant eventually became a teacher of spiritual principles, learning to assist those who had lost their way in life and helping others to overcome their petty hates and grudges (1424-3).

To be sure, trade remained an important aspect of the city's life. The commercial center became a focal point not only for trade but also for large gatherings of people, a variety of laborers, skilled artisans, entertainers, and food vendors. Cayce told a sixty-year-old labor leader that he had purposefully chosen the center of commercial activities as the ideal place to spread his "gospel of good cheer to those who became active in a commercial field . . . " (1354-1) The man presently was a minister of some influence, and he also was informed that his ability to evangelize and sway people to his way of thinking arose from that same Persian experience.

Throughout the city's existence, there were always those—human nature being what it is—who attempted to take advantage of others or pursue opportunities primarily for their own benefit. A twenty-three-year-old college student was told during his reading that he had been among the nomads who challenged Uhjltd's authority, frequently making raids upon caravans to provide for his own livelihood. In his case, however, he eventually came to understand some of the very principles that he had originally disregarded. Most notably, he began to understand the principle of equality and to practice what it suggested about the concept of right and wrong. Soon he was no longer focused on simply meeting his own needs (1528-1).

Eventually, the day came when King Croesus and his never-ending challenges threatened to undermine the normal activities of the city's life. In addition to its spiritual tenets, the proliferation of trade and commerce, and its reputation as a healing center, the city and its traveling caravans became known for being unpredictably (and often unsuccessfully) raided by Croesus's armies. Too often, the king proved himself unable or unwilling to make peace. Finally, Uhjltd used his diplomatic skills to form an alliance with various surrounding settlements and with the wandering nomads between his own city and the kingdom of Croesus. Once the alliance was formed, Uhjltd's army attacked the king's fortress and forced the king to abdicate the throne in favor of his son, Croesus III. About the same time, Ilya found herself pregnant again and later gave birth to a second son. The boy was named Ujndt; as he grew, he became as interested in secular affairs as his brother was in spiritual ones.

During the course of a life reading given in 1936, a sixty-two-year-old wildcat oil driller and philanthropist learned that he had been Croesus III. Worldly-wise and a brilliant conversationalist in the present, he was also interested in helping others, a quality that had been cultivated during his lifetime as the monarch, when he was instrumental in founding schools and places of retreat for young and old. His present-day interest in oil and gas was mirrored in his life as Croesus III because he had been considered progressive in the use of minerals and gas. Although he was a much better king than his father, his desire to remain supreme ruler gave him a dictatorial side that made him "hard upon those who had too many ideas . . . " (1265-3) It was an attitude that needed tempering in the present as well.

In years to come, the presence of oil and gas in the hills and plains around Is-Shlan-doen was instrumental in providing another name for members of the Zoroastrian community. Due to the presence of natural gas vents and the resulting perpetual fires, many of the caves were naturally illuminated. In time, the Zoroastrians used these natural fires for the creation of altars in the worship of their god, Ahura Mazda. It was because of these altars and the ignorance of some people about what the altars represented that others began to call the Zoroastrians "Fire Worshipers."

Friendly interchanges between Is-Shlan-doens and even Croesus II's people were not uncommon. After the abdication of Croesus and his son's assumption of leadership, however, relationships between the two kingdoms became more cooperative in nature. A thirty-one-year-old publicist received a reading in 1935 and learned that he had been among Croesus II's forces defeated when Uhjltd formed the alliance with the neighboring tribes and communities. Rather than being angry or vengeful, however, he became extremely helpful at building ongoing communication between the two cities and eventually came to Is-Shlan-doen to study for himself:

> The entity was among the Persians that had been in and among the officers of the king's command that had been overrun.
>
> The entity came and made for those conditions that brought to its own land a greater peace and harmony, and aided in the establishing of what later became the Zoroastrian activity; which has in the present been of especial interest—and will be more so if it is studied the more. The name then was Axendia.
>
> In the experience the entity gained throughout; and in the present there are those abilities of the entity as to its descriptions that it may write; as of a play, as of a wedding, as of any functioning where there is the activity that joins lives or makes for those associations that will bring into the experience the changes for the opportunity of developing and giving of selves in service for others. These become as innate and manifested in the entity's abilities and activities in the present. It is well to build upon same. 815-2

After the two cities became allies, additional members of Croesus III's immediate family became interested in activities in Is-Shlan-doen. A sixty-four-year-old widow was told that she had been the king's sister and had eventually developed an interest in mysticism and acquainted herself with the various sages who frequented Uhjltd's metropolis. Since she originally was one of the instructors of the young women in the temple school, the time came when she decided to move to Is-Shlan-doen. There, she used her skills to train the young. Cayce informed her that this ability was one of the greatest services she could perform and that it continued to be a part of her life mission in the present (1007-1).

As the city grew and more people began to understand Uhjltd's philosophy, many became teachers and healers in their own right. One of these was named Edssi. He had been among the wealthiest merchants in Croesus II's kingdom and had undoubtedly come to know of Uhjltd's city as a result of trading. After the king's abdication, Edssi decided to make the city of Is-Shlan-doen his home. Perhaps because of his connection to Croesus II, many of those closest to Uhjltd advised extreme caution when dealing with him. Because of his many travels and his years of experience with various cultures, Edssi had a number of ideas that he claimed would help Uhjltd spread his teachings throughout the known world. Although he apparently was sincere, Edssi had a very difficult time convincing anyone else to listen to him.

When a reading was given to the forty-four-year-old executive who had been Edssi, Cayce informed him that, at the time, he had "suffered much in body *and* mind for being doubted." (437-2) Eventually, however, Uhjltd chose to heed his advice and gave Edssi responsibilities that enabled him to further centralize the commercial activities and develop social reforms within the city. With each success, he was given greater and greater authority, until he equaled Esdena as a most trusted advisor. In time, Edssi became second in command of the entire metropolis, serving in the capacity of prime minister or minister of state. In that position, he developed a plan to carry Uhjltd's philosophy and teachings to people throughout the continent. The plan was relatively simple: Is-Shlan-doen would train emissaries and send them to the four corners of the known world.

A reading for a thirty-four-year-old woman stated that she had been one of those who was trained:

> In the one before this we find in that land now known as the Arabian land, and during these periods when there were those gatherings of the peoples about those that had established as of a new kingdom in and about that land, or that place now known as Shushtar. The entity then was among those that gathered there, becoming later—as those periods developed to where emissaries were sent into the various fields, the various lands—the entity then sent to that land from which much of the beauty, the culture, of those in art of the various fields, become as the criterion; for the entity was then *gifted* much in speech, much as an active influence in the establishing of the cultural schools, or that field of endeavor whereby the peoples' time was divided not only in labor, in play, but in the *developing* of the talents *innate* in each individual; becoming the emissary, with its companion, to this Grecian land, or Grecian isle, the entity gained much in this experience . . . 2724-1

In 1935, an eighteen-year-old boy was told that he had once had a Persian lifetime when he was named Cajakan. In that experience, he became one of the emissaries or ambassadors sent to other lands. Because of his activities in that life, he still retained talents for diplomatic service that could be drawn upon in the present. Cayce encouraged him to put those abilities to good use and to pursue an education that would prepare him to become a consul (797-1).

On another occasion, a thirty-four-year-old interior decorator was advised that she had also served as an emissary. Although competent in all lessons that related to healing and the ability to lead a moral and spiritual life, she was often disheartened during her travels. A variety of experiences had lessened her confidence in the ability of individuals and groups to really understand what she was trying to teach them. Thankfully, she eventually found a great deal of success in working with healing, giving much-needed aid to others and finding peace and harmony within herself in the process (2733-1).

The diplomatic work occurring in Is-Shlan-doen was not limited to emissaries traveling to other nations. Frequently, representatives from other regions came to the city to learn what might be useful in their own lands. In 1934, a forty-six-year-old widow learned that she had once been a Chaldean princess who journeyed into the city in an effort to find everything she could that might be of use to her own people:

> The entity was among those of what is now the Persian land, and about the upper Chaldean land. Then the entity was a princess in that land, yet with the preachings, the teachings, the ministerings that were heralded far and near—as to that teacher, that leader in the hills and the plains—the entity journeyed forth with those of its own retinue, of its own kingdom, that there might be gained, as it were, something anew that might be helpful to its own peoples, its own lands.

> Hence in the innate influence in the present from that sojourn we find the more delicate interests the entity-individual has in those that are in political power in the various fields of activity throughout the earth, and as to what impels—or that force behind each of those who are as rulers that motivates

that influence in the lives of the individuals. Not as to the personal, not as to the power, but what is the motivative influence in those that rule.

The entity then was in the name Princess Sunsui; and in that land may there still be seen much of that the entity set as an influence in those people—that has been heralded far and near, as <u>to the ability of these peoples to become more compatible with other individuals and other nations than many</u>. And the interests in the present the entity has in things that partake of the nature from such lands are innate and manifested in its urges. 752-1

On another occasion, an eighteen-year-old student learned that he had gone to the city in the hills and the plains as a representative of the king of the Chaldean lands. He went specifically to learn the tenets that were being taught and to be trained in some of the methods used to make Is-Shlan-doen a model of modernization for its time. Once his training was complete, he returned to Chaldea as a spiritual counselor. His education also enabled him to bring developments in architecture and irrigation back to his nation. In 1935, when the reading was given, Cayce told the young man that archaeological evidence of many of the advancements he had introduced to his country still existed (830-1).

The emissaries sent out by Edssi were <u>not missionaries of specific spiritual dogma</u>. Instead, <u>they were encouraged to help all people bring into their own awareness the knowledge that the influence of Spirit could become a practical experience in everyday life</u>. Their message was not rote; rather, all were encouraged to present in their own way "that which would bespeak the blessings, the benevolent forces of the divine in the activities of men." (516-2)

In other words, Uhjltd taught his people that the Divine was not simply some external being who demanded worship and praise. The presence of God *could* be discovered external to one's self, but more important, the Divine could be found *within*. As people learned to access their own connection to Spirit, they could have a tremendous influence by helping others realize their relationship to the Creator while magnifying the awareness and activity of Spirit in their own lives.

Because the city acted as a gathering point for so many people from other countries, it did much to facilitate the creation of friendships, allegiances, and agreements for peace and mutual prosperity among different cultures. Apparently, people from all walks of life found that they could unite around the ideal that each person was capable of knowing his or her relationship to the Divine and that each was just as important to the Creator.

During the same period that Edssi was rising to a position of authority, a surprising visitor somehow found her way into the city. Emaciated and physically ill, a teenaged girl came to Is-Shlan-doen in search of food and, perhaps, the remnants of her family. The girl was Inxa, daughter of Elia, who had committed suicide, and Oujida, Uhjltd's brother, who had been killed in a desert skirmish. In detailing that period, Cayce told the fifty-two-year-old housewife who had once been Inxa that she had been one of the most beautiful women in the city:

> As a virgin, damsel, the entity then, Inxa, came to this particular place. This about two moons after there was the establishing of the supervision of Edssi [437]. In this place the entity then came under the influence of those in charge there, and the entity was healed from that of emaciation and want by the leader at this place. With the return of health,

strength, and body vitality, that beauty that brought
so many under the influence of the entity was apparent; for the body was then called and considered
the most *beautiful* in body of any that were in this
environ. Especially were the hair and eyes of note,
or interest, to those who came under—what at
times might be called—the spell of the entity. Oft
was there counsel with the leader, or leaders, by the
entity, and the abilities, the influence that the entity had through this association, brought gradually
a wide influence in those directions that became
helpful in every manner to those that aided in dis-
pensing the information, influence, that was had by
these peoples at that particular period. 538-31

According to the readings, in the beginning, Inxa had
a very difficult time living in Is-Shlan-doen. She had
been raised to hate and despise Uhjltd, and she now
found herself completely dependent upon the man she
had been taught for years to scorn. Suspicious of him at
first, she began to form her own opinion of this leader
who was also her uncle. In time she came to recognize
her father's hatred of his brother as a clash of personali-
ties rather than as a legitimate response to this kindly
ruler, whom she would come to love. Inxa was taken in
by Uhjltd and Ilya and became extremely helpful in raising the couple's children. By this time, Ilya had two sons,
Zend and Ujndt, and the couple had also adopted a baby
girl, Uldha, who had been abandoned in the city by her
parents.

It was shortly after Inxa's arrival that Irenan decided
she could no longer remain in the city; perhaps it was
impossible to accept yet another person becoming a
member of Uhjltd's household. Irenan left the metropolis and was not heard from again. According to Cayce, it
was a decision that would haunt her even thousands of

years later, during her life in the twentieth century (295-
1 and 295-9). She had let her jealousy and personal feelings guide her life rather than being guided by the soul
prompting that had brought her to be a part of Uhjltd's
work in the first place.

[margin handwritten notes: motive influences ✳ Future devel.]

Once Inxa overcame her feelings of animosity and
caution toward Uhjltd, she developed a teenage crush
upon the leader, causing her to feel somewhat jealous of
Ilya and the closeness that the couple demonstrated. Ig-
noring the difficulty, Ilya proved extremely patient with
her new charge, never letting the young woman's jealousy affect how Inxa was treated. In a short time, the
older woman's lovingkindness won out, and the two became almost inseparable.

Inxa was much more than just another member of the
household. She came under Ilya's tutelage and became
an integral part of activities in Is-Shlan-doen. More than
simply assisting in the raising of Ilya's children, Inxa
joined Ilya in the healing work of the hospital—an experience that proved very rewarding for both women. The
two also worked together separating travelers to the city
into various groups in order to meet their needs for healing, hospitalization, and teaching. Regardless of the activity, Inxa proved an enthusiastic student. Ilya soon
found that Inxa, wise beyond her years, possessed her
own talents with young people. As a result, she became a
frequent companion and counselor to the children and
teenagers who made the city their home.

In an interesting twist, according to the Cayce readings, the relationship between Inxa and Ilya would be
repeated thousands of years later in a reversal of roles,
when Inxa's twentieth-century counterpart took Ilya into
her home and treated her much like a daughter (538-32
and others).

With the passage of years and the threat of Croesus II
a fading memory, Is-Shlan-doen became one of the most

cosmopolitan cities of its time. In addition to travelers, seekers, and merchants from various lands, a vast mix of people from many cultures took up permanent residency and somehow managed to live in peace. Among the people were Persians, Arabs, and countless members of the nomadic tribes. Others included Chaldeans, Tibetans, and Carpathians. There were also representatives of the various cultures in India, people from the countries of Said and Ur—and, of course, the Greeks. It was these Greeks who began to call Is-Shlan-doen by another name, "Toaz." They also played a major role in determining the future of the city in the hills and the plains.

6

And Then There Were Greeks

With the passage of years, it seemed that Uhjltd fulfilled his destiny in bringing peace to the plains. Is-Shlan-doen proved an ideal place for work that continued to be a tremendous influence on much of the continent and beyond. Whether it was healing, hope, commerce, or a new spiritual way of life, the city attracted seekers from every nation and level of society and sent forth emissaries to share with others what the city's own people had come to know.

While the city matured, Ilya and Uhjltd's three children grew up under the watchful eye of their parents. Zend, Uldha, and Ujndt received special spiritual, mental, and physical training, not only from the couple but also from Inxa, who remained a constant companion. As had been true in his youth, Zend's interest in spirituality continued. He displayed a mystical bent and a zeal that suggested he was to become a great religious leader. Uldha, the couple's adopted daughter, was taught prayer and spiritual healing by her father and became an important part of the city's healing ministry. It was a work of healing that would inspire her, even thousands of years later in her twentieth-century incarnation, when she became a member of Edgar Cayce's original prayer group. In 1931, when she was forty-one years old, the woman who had been Uldha during the Persian period received additional information regarding her activities in that incarnation:

> . . . the entity grew in understanding of how spiritual life may affect the *physical bodies* of peoples *through* the power of prayer and meditation, as *many* were brought to the body's presence for healing in their afflictions; and the body then, through its own efforts, learned again those discernments of who, how, where, the *efforts* of individuals aided one rather than another—see? In *this* manner did the entity advance, and did the entity *learn* prayer, in the sense as it may be applied in raising the continuity of creative consciousness in the minds and hearts of individuals in the present experience, with the abilities for *discernment* through intuitive forces of individuals' activities as respecting the thing sought by others—see? 993-3

The younger boy, Ujndt, showed a propensity for practical leadership, much like his father. Even as a youth, he was able to combine idealism with a depth of wisdom and judgment that seemed beyond his years. A fifty-five-year-old writer and farmer was informed in his life reading that, in ancient Persia, he had been Uhjltd's youngest son. In describing the environment and upbringing that Ujndt experienced, the reading said:

. . . [Is-Shlan-doen] grew from a mere stopping place for the caravans from the east to the west, or from Egypt to Persia, India, and what is now the Mongoloid and Indo-China land.

Hence it gradually became a place of exchange, or as a commercial center, as well as a religious center—as would be termed today, or a place where the healings of many of those afflicted—in various lands—took place.

This brought for the entity in the early period a confusion, yet with the changes wrought there gradually came to be more and more the responsibilities put upon the entity—not merely by the circumstance but the import of the entity then; being that one to whom many came, more and more, for their association and activities with the varied groups.

Thus grew that which is a basic principle in the latent and manifested urge of the entity in the present experience—as to not only the abilities of land areas to be made to produce, but their privilege, and that the opportunity for such should be a part of the activity of those who dwell on or reside in such areas.

For, as the universality of body, mind and soul were the considerations, so were the activities of areas, lands, vegetation, minerals, properties as the product of nature or the soil, to be made and to become a part of this composite experience of the mental, the spiritual, the material developments—as the entity took hold on same. 2091-2

The readings do not state when the first Greek traveler made the journey to Is-Shlan-doen. It is also unclear whether that traveler came in search of trade, healing, or spiritual direction. In all likelihood, the first Greek visi-

tor received exactly what he or she had been in search
of, prompting others to follow. Although many came as
friends, in time the Greeks provided the greatest challenges that the city encountered. As Uhjltd's children
grew to adulthood, this quiet threat began to infiltrate
the city. According to the Cayce readings, as the city grew
in prominence, powerful people in Greece longed to acquire all that Is-Shlan-doen appeared to offer. However,
rather than coming into the metropolis to learn what
they might take back to their homeland, they were
drawn to the idea of taking the city for themselves. The
Greeks began to send spies into the city, at first occasion-
ally and then with greater frequency. Because these spies
mixed easily with other Greek travelers, for a long while
the city and its leaders remained completely ignorant of
the threat.

One of the Greek travelers who arrived in the beginning was named Xuno. Friendly and outgoing, he eventually became acquainted with Inxa. Sometime during
Inxa's twenty-fourth year and after a brief courtship, the
two were married. Xuno joined with his wife in working
with the young people as both instructor and companion. The couple also had the opportunity to help in the
training of Zend and Ujndt, prompting Xuno to eventually became a close friend of the boys' parents.

According to Edgar Cayce, as the years passed, a few
changes did come to the city. In time, both of Uhjltd's
parents died, and Uhjltd and Ilya transferred many of
their previous administrative responsibilities to others.
The two then focused their efforts on the work of healing and on the training and teaching of emissaries and
seekers. Edssi assumed many of the responsibilities of
day-to-day leadership, as well as overall affairs of state.
The ever-loyal Esdena remained a trusted counselor and
advisor, helpful to both Uhjltd and Edssi.

Obviously, many of the Greek travelers and immigrants were ideal citizens and had no idea what some of their fellow countrymen were planning. Among those Greeks truthfully seeking aid was a woman named Zoporo. Although possessing a great artistic talent, she was so weak in body and mind when she came to Is-Shlan-doen that she undoubtedly was not able to use her abilities. After being healed in the hospital, however, she became a part of the schools and taught others how they could preserve stories and history through drawings, sculpture, and even decorations for the home. Also talented in music and song, she eventually helped to document some of the city's activities through musical verse (665-1).

Cayce informed a forty-four-year-old advertising salesman in 1938 that he had been a Greek artisan during that period and had come into the city with only the most honorable of intentions: "The entity then was of the Grecians who came into the land not so much for plunder as to absorb and make those lands a portion of the Grecian experience." (1562-1) Apparently the experience proved even more valuable than he had anticipated. He became a recorder of sorts, documenting in tiles and stones the experiences of many travelers who journeyed into the city for physical, mental, or spiritual aid.

In another case history, a woman was told that she had been a Greek named Eceuda and had traveled to Is-Shlan-doen to learn the spiritual information being taught by Uhjltd. Shortly after, she became an invaluable member of the healing staff, serving as a nurse and bringing harmony to those who suffered from a variety of diseases, whether of the body or of the mind. From that experience, she learned that each person has the opportunity to express their personal concept of the Creator in interactions with others. Innately, she still understood in the twentieth century that it was best to assist others to help themselves—a perspective that Cayce encouraged her to continue working with in the present (1661-2).

There were also those who came in search of *something*—not certain what they were looking for, but finding a purposeful existence in Is-Shlan-doen. During the course of a 1933 reading, a forty-year-old telegraph operator learned that she had been one of those Greeks who had come as a seeker:

> In the one before this we find the entity was in that land now known as the Persian, during those periods when there were the real establishings by great numbers, those that came for the truths that were presented by the teacher in the hills and in the desert land.
>
> The entity then was among those that were called heathen, or of the Grecian land. Hence beauty of body, beauty of thought, the revelling in beautiful expressions—whether they may be presented in the present in sculpture, in paintings, in nature, or in *whatever* form; for *these* were the truths that were made a portion of the entity's experiences in its association with Uhjltd in that experience. For, beauty in all its forms becomes appealing to the entity. 338-2

It was in part because of the Greek emphasis on beauty and the fact that their culture greatly admired the potential beauty of the human form that Is-Shlan-doen began to focus more attention on the physical. Ever since the establishment of the hospital, the city had prided itself on healing and assisting the weak, the lame, and the diseased, but with the arrival of so many Greeks, there began an even greater emphasis on the physical body and personal appearance. The healing regimens practiced at the hospital soon began to consider the

overall development of the physical body. Those considerations included exercise and outdoor activities that
would be appropriate for each person (670-1).

Another Greek, by the name of Edesse, was one of the
first to arrive in the city, coming not only out of curiosity
but also because of her interest in the commercial and
trade possibilities that existed within the city's borders.
Extremely intelligent and beautiful, Edesse saw the value
of the spiritual tenets being taught and wasted no time
in adopting them for herself. She also proved very helpful in making the same information available to those of
many different lands. For that reason, Cayce told her
that, in the present, she found herself attracted to various cultures and peoples and that languages and diplomatic relationships would inevitably come easy to her
(920-1).

Curiosity regarding the city and what it had to offer
was the reason given to a twenty-five-year-old automo-
bile salesman for his own immigration to the city in the
hills and the plains in a past life. The readings told him
that he arrived at a time when the motivation that
seemed to be guiding so many people was one of complete selfishness and personal aggrandizement: "*Today
is! Tomorrow isn't! So live today for all that may be obtained in same.*" (1066-1) His name then was Gargia, and
he wondered why so many people from different lands
continued to be drawn to one "so lowly in life" as Uhjltd.
What he learned was that, somehow, Uhjltd, as a teacher,
was able to instill hope in people, regardless of their life
circumstances. Although he was first driven by curiosity,
Gargia soon decided to remain in the city in order to
study.

The reading pointed out that all of Gargia's motives
had not been pure. Apparently, there had come a time
when he chose to use what he had learned to take advantage of those less intelligent than himself. For that

period of indiscretion, he lost in terms of his soul development. Later, however, he saw what oppression did to people, and he became a champion of personal rights, freedom of speech, freedom of ideas, and the preservation of individual homes. As a result, that period of his life provided him with overall personal development and soul growth.

mistake purposeful

Beyond the Greeks who came as friends and those who arrived in search of something, there were others who were sent into the city solely for invasion and conquest. At first, the plan seemed to be one in which the Greeks were to attempt to seek out economic and political control. More often than not, however, conspiracy plans failed. It was not uncommon for those who had originally been sent into the city in order to gain control of it to become transformed by their experiences instead. The result was that many would-be conspirators decided to become a part of Is-Shlan-doen. A case in point is from a reading given in 1941:

> Before that the entity was in the Persian or Arabian land, when there was the building up of the "city in the hills and the plains," where there was the establishing of those centers of trade along those trade routes from the Indian land, the Mongoloid land, the Caucasian land, and that known as the Tao [?] or the IndoChina land.
>
> The entity was among the Grecians who were sent into that "city in the hills and the plains" in the attempt to undermine the efforts of the teacher there. Yet the entity, coming under the influences of the healing forces, saw the opportunities for material gain by the using of the great influence wrought by the teacher Uhjltd in that city, and thus began to establish closer associations in the efforts and in the endeavors of those groups that passed to

and fro through that city.

Thus the means of exchange, the spices of the east, the linens and the gold from Egypt, the gold as well as the ivory from the IndoChina land, all became a part of the entity's activities through that experience . . .

The name then was Elia—beautiful in body, beautiful in soul through those periods of activity, as it gained through being a helpful force. 2560-1

Deciding to become a part of what the city had to offer was the reason given to many of those who were told they had changed allegiances from Greece to Is-Shlan-doen. During a life reading for a fifty-four-year-old woman, Cayce informed her that she had come into the city for the express purpose of undermining it. Instead, she found a place where people truly lived by the doctrine later expressed as, "Love thy neighbor as thyself." In Is-Shlan-doen, she found that people were given both help and hope, and, as a result, she became one of those who aided Uhjltd and his people rather than subverting them. At the time, her name was Celieo, and she was eventually raised to the position of emissary, becoming a messenger of faith and hope to many countries, including to her former homeland (1599-1).

The experience of being in Is-Shlan-doen inspired people to find purity, wholeness, and personal transformation in their own lives and then encouraged them to reach out to one another. In the process, people found ways to become a part of the healing work, providing comfort to the neglected or those who had been oppressed, or inspiring those who had lost hope. In a very real sense, the city environment provided many with a new life. Another example is the case of a woman who was told that she had arrived with the intent of being a part of the Greek conquest but who changed completely because of what she saw in the city: " . . . hope and love, brotherly kindness and gentleness and patience shown among those where turmoils and strifes so often arose . . . " (1770-2) After becoming a part of the city, she wanted only to truly live in such a manner that she reflected an understanding of each soul's relationship to the Creative Forces. For her efforts, she gained in soul development and found ways to encourage others to achieve their own purposes and abilities. In the process, she gave much to many. Cayce informed her that, in the present, she still possessed the ability to work with the fruits of the Spirit in her interactions with others: love, patience, faith, hope, and kindness.

Just as Croesus II had felt threatened by the city's activities in trade and commerce, the Greeks became jealous of Is-Shlan-doen's growing economic prosperity. Essentially, Uhjltd's tenets regarding both the healing work and the spiritual information were seen by the Greeks as being of little value. It was the lucrative financial opportunities with which they were most concerned. In order to gain control of the material benefits the city offered, they started to send in spies. They believed that propaganda and deception, rather than military force, might conquer the city. The idea was to undermine the spiritual philosophy that seemed to be influencing so many. For that reason, infiltrators were sent in to begin using the very thing against the people that the Greeks had found of no importance to begin with. Shortly thereafter, large numbers of supposed travelers were sent into Is-Shlan-doen, causing the city to be overrun with Greeks.

In 1933, Cayce gave a life reading to a twenty-six-year-old woman and discussed the fact that she had been one of the Greeks to arrive at this period of the city's history. The overall goal of the infiltration was an "attempt to undermine the teachers and the leaders that had begun

with their dissemination of truths in that experience."
(453-1) During that incarnation, she was a very influential man charged with misleading Uhjltd's followers
through deception and trickery. In the beginning, the
plan was successful, and in her Persian incarnation, she
seemed to gain a following among some of the people.
However, Cayce told her that it was not long before she
experienced a change of heart and sought to undo all the
damage she had done. Rather than being a threat against
the city, she eventually become a supporter of all it was
trying to accomplish and used her influence to assist
Uhjltd and his people. Although deciding to become a
part of the city had caused her to lose from a physical
and material perspective, from a mental and spiritual
level, her soul gained much.

A similar experience occurred in the life of a Greek
woman named Mercerces, who was used by her own
people as a pawn in order to gain political and economic
influence. Charged with using her talents to thwart the
activities of some of the city's residents, she rose in position but soon used her notoriety as a means of overin-
dulging in every activity of the flesh. As a result, she
became very ill and was hospitalized before eventually
being healed by Uhjltd himself. Her personal healing led
her to change allegiance, and, in time, she became a
champion for the poor, the homeless, and the city's children who had been abandoned or orphaned. Her efforts
gave much help and joy to others. Cayce encouraged her
to repeat a similar work in the present, providing hope
and encouragement to the helpless and the homeless
(1058-1).

Repeatedly, the Greek plan to overtake the city was
met with one failure after another. Some of the infiltrators were transformed through their personal healings,
and others found much comfort in the spiritual information being taught to the people. Many of the Greeks

were totally unprepared for the influence that the city and its teachers had upon a wide variety of people from other cultures. In addition to all these influences, a number of the Greeks were changed simply by the relationships they developed with the citizens of Is-Shlan-doen. Some even fell in love with other followers of Uhjltd.

Such was the case of a woman named Pegesus, who arrived to undermine the city's activities. In the course of her wanderings in the city, she became acquainted with Elhasen, one of Uhjltd's brothers and the same soul who was her husband in the present. Eventually, the acquaintance led to romance, and the two were married. From that day forward, she became a helpful influence, especially in the hospital. The focus of her work was with the aged, the indigent, the mentally confused, and the physically crippled. Because of her sincerity and her talents, the readings suggest that her efforts had caused her to become something of a celebrity in the city. In time, Pegesus served as one of the greatest advocates for the sick (808-18).

When it became exceedingly clear that the Greeks were not achieving the influence they desired, a new, more dangerous effort was conceived. They decided to take over the city through a direct confrontation with the people's spiritual and religious convictions, destroying their moral character in the process. The plan was simple; by various means, the Greeks pulled together 368 of the most beautiful women in their country to journey to Is-Shlan-doen (2487-1). Although most of the women came of their own free will, others arrived through coercion and force. All of the Greek maidens who had been recruited entered the city, under the guise of dancers and entertainers. Their real purpose, however, was to seduce the most influential men in the metropolis, an art in which all of them had been trained.

It was not long before the leaders of Is-Shlan-doen realized what was occurring. Esdena was one of the first to recognize the potential danger. At first, he counseled that the best means of solving the problem was by reaching out to the women in peace. In this manner, they might be convinced—like so many other Greeks—that the city had something of value to offer them personally. When some of the women used Esdena's overtures toward them as a means of attempting seduction, he decided that the women needed to be under constant surveillance and that all of the city's citizens should be alerted to the threat. He also suggested calling upon neighboring countries such as the lands of Egypt, the Caucasus, and India for assistance—even going so far as to use women themselves as a means of bringing foreign warriors to their aid. This idea did not get Uhjltd's approval.

Esdena was not the only person concerned over the danger posed by so many threatening Greeks. As political leader, Edssi was also very much alarmed. The only question was one of the proper course of action. By this time, Uhjltd's sons had grown to adulthood and had assumed leadership roles as well. As a result of the infiltration of Greek women, disagreements arose between the two brothers because they held differing opinions about how best to oppose the threat. Zend believed that the best response was spiritual passivity, thwarting the women's plans while they came under the influence of the beliefs that held the city together. Conversely, although Ujndt insisted on maintaining the city's spiritual foundation, he counseled a more concrete defense such as that proposed by Esdena.

During the course of a reading given to the person who had been Ujndt in the Persian period, Cayce discussed this period of the city's history and the growing division between Uhjltd's two sons:

In the latter part of Uhjltd's sojourn in that particular period of activity, the entity then—Uhjntd
[Ujndt]—having reached manhood—at the age of
thirty-one years, as would be termed today, had to
cope with the activities just beginning from the Grecian land—first the attempts of the Grecians to use
the groups of girls, or women, as a means to undermine those activities in the "city in the hills and the
plains," by their form or manner of entertainment
and associations.

From those attempts grew those differences of
the entity with the associate or companion, or
brother, Zend, as to the spiritual and the material
activities.

Thus gradually there grew a division from those
disturbances, during the latter days of Uhjltd, so
that—as would be described in present day par-
lance—one held to the theory [Zend] that only
spiritual passiveness should be the activity of man;
the other [Ujndt] held that there should be the practical application of spiritual, mental *and* material
needs to meet the law of the nature of man—or
natural sources.

These divisions gradually grew so that there became adherents to each group; not only in the city
or land about the "city in the hills and the plains"
but from other groups that were gradually fostered
from the teachings in other lands—the Egyptian,
portions of Northern Persia, the Indian, the land of
On or the Mongoloid, also Tau [?]—as in the Indo-
China land. All of these played or had their part in
producing the divisions that *eventually* brought the
undermining of those who held to the principles of
the one, and to the purposes and principles of the
other.

The entity then, Uhjndt [Ujndt], held to the belief that the spiritual influences were to be a practical application in the mental and the material life, and that they were to be a part of *every* individual, as individuals, and in the same manner in principle applied to the associates of *any* individual, in dealing with influences or forces from without—that is, the *same* principles applied in the manner necessary to deal with influences from without; as in the attempted invasion, which later became—as would be termed—a military expedition from Greece.

There the entity desired to defend, and to make for that activity necessary—not of a warlike nature but of a spiritual, mental *and* material defense against same.

On the other hand, the groups of Zend (later known as the Zoroastrian groups) pushed on away from same.

Thus we find the entity holding to those principles that had been demonstrated in the manner in which the groups of maidens were sent first as the undermining influence, so that these in the most part were made to become a determining factor for good.

So did the entity in those abilities as the leader, as the director of the activities, turn the earlier portion of such attempted invasions to good; and not as an appeasement for the departure from principles, as would be termed today, but the ability to coordinate physical, mental and spiritual *as* the principles had been handed from the teachings of Uhjltd. 2091-2

According to the reading, the city also was forced to deal with a number of other opposing forces after the arrival of the Greek women. In addition to the differing perspectives about how the threat the women presented should be addressed, many of Is-Shlan-doen's citizens suddenly found themselves faced with appealing diversions and enticements that conflicted with the beliefs and purposes they claimed to be about. Rather than focusing only on healing, their involvement with service, or the spiritual practices of meditation and prayer, they found various types of entertainment suddenly available that often conflicted with the timing of their previous pursuits. Even in the beginning, the temptation proved too much for some.

Edgar Cayce told a fifty-one-year-old attorney that, although he was one of those who had strongly supported the city, the seduction by the Greek entertainers led him astray. In that incarnation, he came into Is-Shlan-doen from the kingdom of Croesus and helped to establish commercial and social interchanges between the two cities. Heavily influenced by Uhjltd, he eventually rose to a position of power and influence making him one of the targets of the Greek maidens after their arrival. Their beauty proved too much for him, causing both his body and mind to be overcome—at least for a time (816-3).

The women had the ability to sway not only the citizens of Is-Shlan-doen, but also some of their own countrymen as well. A number of Greeks who had been friendly to the city suddenly changed their allegiances due to the efforts of the women. A thirty-six-year-old man was told that he was a Greek and gave way to "self-indulgencies and self-aggrandizements" after the arrival of his own people. He came into the city as a merchant during the city's early growth and chose to stay after coming under the influence of the people and their beliefs. His personal conversion was forgotten, however, and he reverted to selfishness, placing his physical desires and material concerns above the things he had come to believe. The reading encouraged him in the present to reapply the things he once learned, placing others' needs above his own and finding a means of being of service (366-5).

Although this plan of subversion was successful to some extent, once again the Greeks underestimated the city's transformational power and the influence that Uhjltd and his teachings were to have upon the conspirators after their arrival. In 1938, a twenty-two-year-old actress learned during the course of her life reading that she had been one of the seductive maidens sent into the city. Rather than influencing the men, however, she was transformed:

> The entity was among those of the Grecians that were chosen because of the beauty of body, the beauty in form, and because of the abilities in the activities to represent that which would make for the drawing away from those activities that had been presented by Uhjltd in that land of the Persians and the Arabians.
>
> Then the entity came into the Arabian or Persian lands, or "the city in the hills and the plains," and there the activities were to draw away the activities of those peoples from the religious thought and cults rather to the beauty for the satisfying of the individual appetites and activities in the experience.
>
> Yet with those changes that came about, with the entity entering into the teachings of the leader Uhjltd in those experiences there were brought many changes. And though the entity was termed as one who had become as a renegade to the purposes of its own land, yet the entity in the beauty of its person, in the beauty of its abilities gave to the peoples of many lands that concept of the use of beauty, the use of grace, the use of activities that

induced those of other fields of service to become closer associated with the spiritual thoughts.

Thus the entity gained and lost, and gained, and grew in those periods to become one that was called in those days the Princess of the Temple in dancing, posing, and in making for those activities in the services there.

The name then was Aphade. 1510-1

She was not the only maiden to be positively affected by the city. Edgar Cayce told several people that they were among the Greek women and that they were changed by their experiences in the city in the hills and the plains. Many were told that they set aside their powers of seduction and, instead, used their beauty to become a helpful influence. Although some continued to use their talent for entertainment in a manner appropriate to their change of heart, others became healers, teachers, storytellers, translators, artists, nurses, and even ministers, helping to spread the city's spiritual tenets.

The transformative power of Is-Shlan-doen was not limited to the Grecian maidens. Even one of the men who was sent in with the women as a trainer and guide found himself coming under Uhjltd's influence. Afterward, he forsook his plans of treachery and, according to the readings, "applied self just in making the corner where it was more like the paradise or haven of God." (3376-2) Cayce told the present-day woman who was a man in that incarnation that, during the experience, she accomplished much because she recorded many of the spiritual tenets which were handed down to Uhjltd's sons to assist those who came after.

On another occasion, a twelve-year-old boy was told that he was also among the helpful Greeks and made Is-Shlan-doen his home. In that incarnation, he attempted to stop the subversion that was being undertaken by some of his countrymen. Rather than seeing only the commercial possibilities offered by the city, he came to know firsthand the spiritual and emotional help that was available. Although somewhat torn by doubt and fear over turning against his fellow Greeks, he decided that the ideals of the city were much more important than his allegiance to his former country (1123-1). Apparently, his feelings and his response to the infiltration were not isolated reactions. For that reason, the Greek plan to control the city appeared on the verge of collapse.

Rather than giving up, however, the Greeks decided that, for their next course of action, they would launch an all-out military assault.

7

The End of What Was

According to the Cayce readings, the ongoing difficulties that Is-Shlan-doen experienced with the
Greeks proved especially disappointing to Ilya. At her
age and after more than four decades of effort directed
toward Is-Shlan-doen, she hoped that the work she and
her husband had begun would no longer be beset with
challenge. In spite of the difficulties, however, her life
was good overall. She lived to see her children grown and
married, each established in his or her own way. Uldha
continued her work with the hospital and healing. Inxa
remained a part of their extended family and still pur-
sued her efforts with young people. Both Ilya's sons became leaders in their own right—one focused on theology
and spirituality, the other on trying to combine spiritual
principles into the politics of protecting a major city. She
had every reason to be satisfied with her life and to be

proud of what she and her husband accomplished.

Uhjltd became a legendary figure, even in his own time. He was venerated for his wisdom, for his healing abilities, and for being the central figure in transforming an abandoned desert outpost into one of the most notable Persian cities of its day. Even considering the threat of the Greek presence, he did much to bring peace to the plains. Many of the scattered people eventually joined with the city, and the nomadic tribes who continued to wander the desert no longer warred with one another.

Uhjltd also gave his people a new philosophy of life, one that championed service and self-improvement rather than dominion over others. As a result, he was sought out by counselors and diplomats from throughout the known world and became to Persia what Ra Ta had been to Egypt 2,000 years previously. His words and tenets were recorded and, eventually, became the basis for many of the principles disseminated by Zend and, later, by Zend's son, Zarathustra. Taken together, this information would form the early foundation of the Zoroastrian faith. With the passage of years, Uhjltd relinquished most of the city's governance to others. In addition to teaching and healing, much of his time was now spent with his wife and his family.

Edssi still led the city's general administrative affairs, but the overall responsibility of protecting the citizens of Is-Shlan-doen from possible threat fell to Ujndt. For a long while, Uhjltd's youngest son was able to prevent an actual outbreak of hostilities. He managed to divert the ongoing Greek influence into positive directions and, somehow, to encourage a conversion of the Greeks to an acceptance of the city's spiritual principles along the lines that had been proposed by Zend. Rumors of a greater threat persisted, however, causing the rift between the two brothers to widen as each posed different approaches for dealing with the danger. Making the dif-

ferences between the two even greater was the fact that
each of them had supporters and led separate portions
of the citizenry. For some, it appeared that, even if the
Greek threat did not manage to undermine the city, the
growing separation between the two brothers might.

Gertrude
see p. xii

Ujndt and Zend were not the only members of Uhjltd's
family having problems. For a long while, Inxa had been
having her own difficulties with Xuno, her husband. Apparently, he was swayed by some of his former countrymen and became convinced that much that the Greeks
hoped to do in the city was justifiable. At best, his opinion caused a great deal of friction in his marriage; at
worst, it appeared as the act of a traitor. Although it cannot be conclusively determined from the Cayce information, in all likelihood Xuno was used as a pawn. He was
probably the person responsible for getting Uhjltd and
Ilya to leave the city just prior to a planned assault by the
Greeks, convincing the couple to leave under the guise
of having them take a much-needed sabbatical. He may
not have clearly understood what was to follow.

What is known is that Uhjltd and Ilya decided to make
a pilgrimage to the old kingdom of Croesus II. Although
the trip might have included a meeting with Croesus III,
possibly to discuss the ongoing relationship between the
two cities, the primary purpose of the journey was to al-
low Ilya to return to the place of her childhood. The readings state that, during the couple's visit to the Persian
court, a Greek assassin murdered both Ilya and Uhjltd at
a time exactly corresponding to the Greek raid upon Is-
Shlan-doen. Ilya was knifed just below her left breast,
and Uhjltd was stabbed on his right side. The two died in
the very place that Ilya had been educated as a child. In
addition to their deaths, those wounds left a deep impression on their physical bodies, resulting in birth-
marks that each possessed even into the twentieth
century. Cayce stated:

... they each bear in the body at present a mark designating these conditions. On the female body, just below the left breast, to the side and on the edge of breast itself, the mark, and an answering one on the body of the male, in the opposite proximity of the breast . . . 288-6

Gladys Davis p xii

The assassination left a lasting soul memory in each, causing Uhjltd's twentieth-century counterpart to be distrustful of friendships—after all, hadn't Xuno convinced them to make the trip?—and Ilya's counterpart to have a dreadful fear of knives.

Meanwhile, back in Is-Shlan-doen the attack on the city was devastating. The Greeks gathered their armed warriors and hired mercenary patrols. The assault was swift and violent, and its effects were far-reaching. Edssi was killed during the attack, just one of the city's many followers who died. With his death and the death of Uhjltd, the entire city was thrown into confusion. After the first phase of the attack and the probable establishment of a Greek military presence, Inxa convinced Uldha and Ujndt to follow her into exile. Zend was also encouraged by one of his followers by the name of Iahn to gather many of the records so that, regardless of what transpired, the spiritual tenets could be reestablished in another portion of the land. Zend and his son followed Iahn's counsel and went into exile as well. *Zarathustra*

The Cayce readings do not provide many details regarding what happened after the initial attack on the city. In time, the Greeks were overthrown and the people of Is-Shlan-doen attempted to recapture what had been lost. Unfortunately, because of the death or departure of many of those who had been in charge, several people competed to lead the city. According to Cayce, Uhjltd's brother, Elhasen, proved an extremely helpful influence at this period by holding things together until Ujndt

could return (2784-1). The Greek attack caused problems among the local nomadic tribes as well. One of the
chieftains used the occasion to bring some of the tribes
together, take for himself the name "Uhjltd the Second,"
and begin to randomly punish anyone who might have
had any involvement in the assault (2709-1).

Ujndt did return and finally assumed complete leadership responsibilities. Zend and some of his followers
decided to pursue a different course of action, however,
and established a new city in another part of the country
to provide a second place of refuge to desert travelers.
Apparently the differences between the two brothers
and their followers had become too great. Together, they
could not effectively govern what remained of Is-Shlan-
doen.

The Greek attack caused much damage to the city's
crops and fields. With Ujndt's return, in addition to rees-
tablishing peace and order within the city, one of his first
orders of business was to focus attention on the produc-
tion of food for the populace. Through his efforts, Ujndt
was able to make even barren lands into productive
fields. In a relatively short period of time, the supply of
food became plentiful, and storehouses were set aside
to hold the surplus.

After Ujndt became the undisputed leader, Inxa was
also elevated to a position of responsibility. Evidently
because Xuno was tricked into taking part in the Greek
attack, she eventually reconciled with her husband, although she was never quite able to completely trust him
again. In discussing this phase of her life in that incarnation, Cayce informed the fifty-two-year-old woman who
had been Inxa that she lived for a long time after the city's
rebirth:

Gertrude ?

   The entity, as we find, remained in this surrounding, this environ; for eventually the companion was

gradually won back, yet never occupying the important place or position, never trusted by the entity
nor the leaders, through the rise of those lessons
that were given which became the foundations of
many of those places of refuge that were established by the emissaries, which would today be
called the schools for the prophets [Essenes?].

The entity lived to be a hundred and twenty years
of age, as would be termed in the present day reck-
oning, retaining the strength, the vitality of the
body, through the whole period. When *choosing* to
give over those activities to that one, and those, who
had been trained, simply closed the eyes—and
rested. 538-32

Ever faithful, Esdena remained an integral part of the
city. He also made journeys to the new city of Zend and
shared what he had come to know of "clean living as to
the relationships of the soil, of the air, of the sun, of the
water . . . " (826-4) In time, he was honored for his insights. Evidently, much of his information eventually
became part of the Zoroastrian philosophy, and Esdena
himself lived to the amazing age of 178!

Although the height of Is-Shlan-doen's glory was over,
in one respect, the end of what had been gave birth to
the beginning of what would be in a variety of ways.
Moreover, the city continued to have a lasting effect
upon the desert, its people, and even on the lands beyond. For a long while, it continued to exist as a stopping
point for travelers. It offered rest, healing, trade, and an
understanding of spiritual principles that was perhaps
unsurpassed on earth. Whether people came in search
of needs for their body, mind, or soul, they found what
they sought in the city in the hills and the plains. The
work of the city's emissaries and diplomats had also
done much to disseminate these same truths to coun-

tries far beyond Persia and its borders.

It is not known when the city disappeared beneath the sands of time or whether this period actually laid the groundwork for what would become the Persian Empire of recorded history. What is known is that the impact of this period for all the souls who were a part of Is-Shlan-doen remained an important soul influence on those who had twentieth-century lives thousands of years later. From the perspective of the Edgar Cayce readings, it is also clear that the Persian era provided yet another occasion for a number of souls to continue their work together of transforming the consciousness of the world.

The work that began in Atlantis moved next to ancient Egypt at the time of Ra Ta. Its influence reappeared in Persia, during the founding of Is-Shlan-doen, before moving on to Palestine at the time of the Christ. Finally, that work incarnated during the lifetime of Edgar Cayce, in an activity that was destined to change human thinking in many directions. Ultimately, the story of Uhjltd is but one chapter in an ongoing saga of a work that continues to transform our understanding of who we are and what we should be about.

8

The Birth of Zoroastrianism

In spite of the fact that hundreds of readings discuss the Uhjltd period and ancient Persia, Cayce's explanation of the entire impetus that gave birth to the Zoroastrian religion is sketchy at best. What is known is that the spiritual tenets that formed the foundation of life in Is-Shlan-doen were recorded and later disseminated, especially by Zarathustra, whom the Greeks called Zoroaster. According to the readings, Zoroaster was the son of Zend and the person most responsible for making certain that these tenets survived, especially through his own extensive missionary wanderings.

In 1935, during the course of a life reading given to a thirty-nine-year-old rabbi, Cayce said that the man had been one of the scribes who worked closely with Uhjltd. The ideas he recorded then eventually enabled others to extract from the information that which would benefit them in their own personal experience. He was encouraged to continue working with the application of spiritual principles, enabling him to recapture some of the benefit of that Persian experience and to bring a greater sense of harmony into his own life and the lives of others. Cayce explained the rabbi's experience in that incarnation:

Before that we find the entity was in the land now known as the Persian or Arabian, about that city builded in the "hills and the plains," about that *now* known as or called Shushtar in Persia or Arabia.

These were the dwelling places then of the entity with the teacher that had builded there. Hence those teachings that arose through the grandson of Uhjltd [294], or Zoroastrianism, have a peculiar intent in the experiences of the entity. And those ritualistic forms that arise from the legends and stories of same bear upon the entity in the present.

For the entity aided rather as what may be termed now the scribe with Uhjltd in that experience; being of the Persians who came to join in the activities there, for the entity was then healed in body through the influences of Uhjltd, the teacher.

Hence to the various individuals who came, the entity then—as Ajhdltn, or Hjltdn—acted not exactly as a priest, but as a recorder of those things that might aid them in bringing in their *own* environ, in their *own* surroundings, a more harmonious experience; no matter from what environ they may have come for those teachings, whether pertaining to the commercialization of activity from the east and the west or from India to Egypt, or from the southern portion of Araby or Arabia or Iran, or from the peoples that were then of the Mongoloids to the Carpathians, to those of the sea. The entity then was the one who gave the instructions as outlined by the teacher in that experience.

In the present may the entity make the greater application of that experience, personally, in the material things of this life, as a teacher, as a lecturer, that would _coordinate_ the teachings, the philosophies of the east and the west, the oriental and the occidental, the new truths and the old. For, as the sage of old gave, "There is nothing new under the sun." But a new setting may be given by the entity as to What Is Truth, that may be binding upon the hearts and minds and upon the experiences of all that will hear.

These are the lessons, these are the truths, the tenets upon which the entity may build harmony into its own experience, and into the experiences of others. 991-1

On another occasion, a twenty-nine-year-old woman learned that she had also been a scribe during the same period. Her present-day abilities as a writer were traced to that experience, when she was a record keeper of some of the spiritual tenets that later formed the Zoroastrian faith. She was single at the time of her reading in 1944, but her reading implied that her husband in that incarnation would, in all likelihood, become her husband in the present:

Before that the entity was in what is now known as the Grecian, Persian and Arabian land. For the entity was among the Grecians, beautiful in body, purposeful in activities, being an entertainer who could use the wiles to influence men as well as its own associates and companions; being among those sent to the "city in the hills."

There the entity came in contact with the associ-

ates and the companion of Uhjltd, that brought
about changes in its experiences in the earth. For
the entity accepted the tenets and teachings of the
healer, the teacher there.

There the entity met and became associated with
the companion who should be the companion in
this experience. May it be so. For the entity brought
the teachings, the instructions, the abilities to write,
from those experiences.

For the entity then was the keeper of the records
for what became the Zoroastrian religious purposes. 3685-1

Although Zoroaster enabled the spiritual movement
of Zoroastrianism to survive by continuing the missionary work begun by the emissaries from Is-Shlan-doen,
Cayce said that it was Zend who originally compiled the
information that formed the Zend-Avesta, the Zoroastrian Bible. Interestingly enough, the readings say that
Zend was none other than an early incarnation of the
same soul who would eventually be born as Jesus. Rather
than being concerned with matters of religious dogma,
the readings say this soul consistently was involved, either directly or indirectly, with every religious movement
that held to the principle of the oneness of God. In discussing the involvement in so many different faiths of
the soul who was Jesus, the readings say that the impelling spirit behind each of them was really one and the
same:

Whether in Buddhism, Mohammedanism, Con-
fucianism, Platoism, or what—these have been
added to much from that as was given by Jesus in
His walk in Galilee and Judea. In all of these, then,
there is that same impelling spirit. What individuals have done, do do, *to* the principles or the spirit

of same—in turning this aside to meet their *own* immediate needs in material planes, or places has made for that as becomes an outstanding thing, as a moralist or the head of any independent religious force or power; for, as has been given, "Know, O Israel, the Lord thy God is *one!*" whether this is directing one of the Confucius' thought, Brahman thought, Buddha thought, Mohammedan thought . . . Because there are contentions, because there is the lack of the giving and taking as to others' thought, does not change God's attitude one whit; neither does it make one above another; for, as has been given, there *is only* one . . . "He that loves me will keep my commandments." What are the commandments? "Thou shalt have no other *God* before me," and "Love thy neighbor as thyself." In this is builded the whole *law* and gospel of every age that has said, "There is *one* God!" 364-9

The period of Is-Shlan-doen was actually a time in the history of the world when people came to understand the need to apply spiritual truths in everyday life. Cayce said that this understanding enabled individuals to make great strides in their personal development, while also becoming a constructive influence on the lives of others. According to the readings, for the first time in that part of the world, a city taught the brother-sisterhood of humankind and that God is the spiritual parent of every individual. This philosophy distinguished it from all other Persian communities and became part of the impetus for its growth into a center of healing and learning. These teachings also included an emphasis on what would later be termed the fruits of the spirit.

A fifty-two-year-old woman who lived at the time of Uhjltd was told what those fruits of the spirit were:

Fruits of the Spirit or 7

As has been given, the *fruits* of Life, or of the
Spirit, are love, long-suffering, patience, understanding, brotherly love, preference of others before self, and the like; while hate, contention, and
the such, are the fruits of those that are destructive
in their elements, and all should refrain from such.
538-32

Later, these spiritual principles evolved into the Zoroastrian emphasis on the importance of each person's efforts to make spiritual virtues a part of his or her life. Zoroastrianism encourages religious virtue, truthfulness,
purity, generosity to the poor, and being mindful of ex-
emplifying good words, good thoughts, and good deeds.
On the other hand, the "sins" from which each person
must refrain include heresy, untruthfulness, perjury,
sexual excess, violence, and tyranny.

In contrast to the Cayce readings, traditional history
holds that Zoroaster was born in 660 B.C. and died in 583
B.C. Tradition also states that Zoroaster was an earnest
seeker of truth and received his vision at the age of thirty.
According to legend, it was Zoroaster who compiled the
Zend-Avesta after his visionary encounter with six archangels and an experience of direct communication with
God. Originally, the Zoroastrian scriptures that the
prophet compiled consisted of twenty-one nasks (books),
but because of the destruction of the Persian Empire by
Alexander the Great, only one of these, the *Vendidad,* is
believed to have survived.

The Zend-Avesta is not only Zoroastrianism's scripture
(Avesta) but also its religious law and the interpretation
of both. Legend also says that two copies of these sacred
texts were inscribed upon 12,000 ox hides by order of
King Vishtaspa, Zoroaster's first important convert.
These copies were to serve as the standard texts of the faith
as the religion was disseminated throughout the world.

The Avesta eventually was translated into several other languages, including Syrian, Aramaic, Hebrew, and Greek.

Although not considered a unique "son of God," Zoroaster was believed to have been sent to the earth to spread his religious doctrine and to do a particular work. His religion was built upon the love of the earth and its bounty, the worship of one God, an ethical code of conduct toward all others, and the healing goodness of being productive in life. Zoroaster also taught and stressed the individuality of each person and each person's responsibility toward the universe. He believed that the powers that manifested in all creation and in nature itself are the gifts of the one God, Ahura Mazda, the one Universal Force. This was demonstrated to the people by their dependence upon the elements of the soil, water, sun, and air, providing sustenance for their physical bodies. Through emissaries, these tenets were taken to many parts of the world, making the Zoroastrian faith the world's first missionary religion. Eventually, however, the missionary focus was discontinued.

Zoroastrians believe that the introduction of Ahura Mazda was the first time in any religion where a universal, loving Father-God is the only God. He is the father of good thoughts, the Creator of all, and a personal God who can be father-brother-friend. By following a life of virtue, Ahura Mazda offers eternal immortality in his kingdom.

Part of the appeal of Zoroastrianism is the fact that the faith is open to all. The religion is also extremely optimistic; regardless of a person's past, there is always the possibility of repentance and change.

In essence, Zoroastrianism is very much concerned with humanity's use of free will to align with Spirit. Although each person is ultimately a creature of Ahura Mazda, because of the nature of free will, he or she can also place him- or herself on the side of the evil spirit,

Ahriman. For the Zoroastrian, light and darkness, truth and falsehood, and right and wrong are forever struggling for supremacy. This tenet means that time can be divided into three periods: the original Creation, when everything was perfect; the present, in which there is the existence of the forces of good and evil; and the future, when perfection will be restored.

In time, the Zoroastrian faith exercised a considerable influence on Judaism, Christianity, and Islam. What these faiths have in common is a belief in good and evil, angels, Judgment Day, the resurrection of the body, and an afterlife in which the ultimate goal is Paradise. The Zoroastrians also speak of the coming of a Messiah (Saoshyant) who will lead the battle between the forces of good and evil, ultimately proving victorious.

In addition to emphasizing truthfulness, kindness, justice, benevolence, devotion to God, and the doing of good works, for centuries the Zoroastrians also once placed much importance on agriculture. In fact, agriculture was held in higher regard by the religion than even prayer. Apart from the obvious necessity of feeding the people, another reason for its elevation was that one's crops could be seen, whereas one's innermost thoughts could not. For the same reason, a person's home and family continue to be considered important outward demonstrations of one's inner faith.

Other Zoroastrian beliefs include the sacredness of the elements of earth, water, and fire, and that none are to be defiled in any way. Because of this belief, it is forbidden to simply bury the dead. Instead, the Zoroastrian dead are placed on "towers of silence" so the corpses can be exposed to the sun while vultures and other predatory birds consume the flesh. Later, any remaining bones may be buried. In addition to being a sacred element, fire is also venerated as the highest and purest symbol of the Divine.

As an illustration of the Zoroastrian faith's eventual influence on other religions, Edgar Cayce told a forty-two-year-old electrical engineer that he had been a Jew in Chaldea. At the time, he joined with others who had incorporated the spiritual understandings handed down from "the old Persian teacher, Zoroaster" (1297-1) into the faith of their forefathers.

Regardless of the actual date of its origins, the Zoroastrian faith proved a tremendous influence in uniting the Persian people through a number of periods in their history. This fact becomes even more impressive when one considers that the Iran of today is only a portion of what once constituted the Persian Empire. At its height, the empire covered such vast regions as Persia, Media, Chaldea, Elam, Babylonia, Assyria, the highlands of Armenia, northeastern Arabia, and even portions of Egypt.

One final note regarding Zoroastrianism is mentioned by the Cayce information. According to the readings, the Persians were gifted in their understanding of the study of the heavens and the celestial bodies. This understanding prompted at least three Zoroastrian Wise Men to make a journey into Bethlehem to see for themselves the birth of the One foretold by the stars. In 1939, a forty-nine-year-old science editor was informed that he had been one of the Wise Men, a student of astrology and Zoroastrianism, and the very one to have brought incense to the infant Jesus (1908-1).

Afterword

Apart from the fact that Edgar Cayce discussed the existence of Is-Shlan-doen, the city in the hills and the plains, in hundreds of readings, can we really give credence to a story that, thus far, has no historical or archaeological evidence? Actually, the fact that a city could disappear from the annals of recorded history and yet remain a part of legend is not without precedent. For centuries, Homer's *Iliad* and *Odyssey* were generally viewed as largely fictional accounts from antiquity that had little basis in fact. Although based, in part, on traditional history, Homer's epics of the Trojan Wars were seen as the independent creation of one or more poets who composed the materials sometime around the eighth century B.C. on the west coast of Asia Minor.

Just as Cayce's story of Is-Shlan-doen revolves around the activities and influence of a central character and a few prominent individuals, Homer's epics detailing the celebrated city of Troy are generally concerned with the life, battles, and wanderings of the Greek heroes Achilles and Odysseus. For more than 2,000 years, Homer's characters and his city of Troy were regarded as legendary with no basis in historical fact. That view changed completely in 1870, however, when German archaeologist Heinrich Schliemann (1822-1890) began excavations that unearthed the stone walls of an ancient city not too far distant from the Aegean Sea and the Dardanelles, just where legend—and Homer—had placed the city of Troy.

Although Schliemann's formal education ended as a teenager, even as a young man he displayed a fascination with Homeric legend and desired to prove its historical authenticity through archaeology. Starting work in a grocery store, he eventually became a successful businessman and world traveler before immigrating to the United States. At the age of twenty-eight, he became a U.S. citizen and, by the time he was forty, he had amassed a fortune. It was at that point that he decided to retire in order to pursue his dream of discovering Homer's Troy.

Schliemann began excavations in Turkey on the hillside of Hissarlik. His work uncovered the existence of several ruins of ancient cities, and he eventually proclaimed that the second city from the bottom was that of Homeric Troy. Later work by additional archaeologists suggested that Homer's Troy was at a higher level and that the place called Hissarlik ("place of fortresses") actually contained the ruins of at least nine settlements of Troy. These excavations suggested that the Troy of the *Iliad* and the *Odyssey* had existed and was destroyed by fire around the early twelfth century B.C., a time corresponding to the traditional date of the Trojan War. Today, archaeologists believe that the war may have resulted because of the Greeks' desire to plunder the city's wealth and put an end to Troy's commercial control of the Dardanelles, a theory that provides an interesting corollary to Cayce's account of the reason behind the Greek infiltration of Is-Shlan-doen.

The only information that we have today regarding the whereabouts of Is-Shlan-doen is Cayce's reference to the fact that Uhjltd's cave was located seven and one-quarter miles southwest of the city of Shushtar. The accuracy of that information might be verified by sending additional excursions to follow the trail of the 1970s' expeditions by Bill and Elsie Sechrist, Hugh Lynn Cayce, and others who believed they found a possible site. Beyond that information, there are only a few additional reading references about the existence of relics in the area:

- In 1930, a forty-year-old housewife was told that she had been one of the maidens from the city of Croesus II who had been captured by Uhjltd's people. Eventually, she ended up in Is-Shlan-doen. After her death, she was entombed in one of the caves in the area. The reading says that her body from that lifetime could still be found, along with others who had been buried at about the same time (454-2).
- A thirty-five-year-old naturopathic physician was told in 1934 that she had been an Egyptian and had journeyed to Is-Shlan-doen, becoming a part of life in the city. Perhaps because of her Egyptian background, her work included the preparation of bodies for burial. She apparently left records of Uhjltd's spiritual tenets with the bodies for which she was responsible. She was told by the reading that those records still exist in the form of tablets containing symbols as well as some of the spiritual information disseminated by the city (500-1).
- During the course of a life reading given in 1927, Cayce advised a thirty-five-year-old man that he had

been a just tax collector during the ancient Persian period. He was a lover of tapestries, fine linen, apparel, and clothing, and remnants of some of his belongings were still located in a cave twelve miles southeast [southwest?] of the city of Shushtar (2734-1).

• A thirty-one-year-old travelers' aide was informed that, in her Persian incarnation, she rose to the position of priestess. She was active in the establishment of places of worship, and some of the materials she once used in the creation of altars still existed as ruins in 1934 (603-1).

• A thirty-two-year-old man involved in the radio business was told in 1930 that he had been a devoted servant and aide to King Croesus II. Because of his devotion to Croesus, he apparently built a memorial honoring the power and might of the king, a memorial that still existed in the hill country just southeast of Shushtar. Cayce went on to tell him that, in the same location, there was also a great cache of gold (2738-1).

• In 1935, a fifty-two-year-old widow was advised that she had been one of the record keepers for Uhjltd and that evidence of her records—as well as some additional treasures from the same period—still existed in the caves just outside of present-day Shushtar (892-1).

Although interesting, the information in the Cayce readings remains anecdotal until evidence of the city is found. Taking into account Edgar Cayce's accuracy in so many other areas, is it possible that his information on Is-Shlan-doen is an accurate depiction of real people and events? Since his death, much of the Cayce information has been repeatedly checked and verified. There have also been numerous occasions when even his ability to peer into the past has been validated. For example, in a number of readings (364-13, 276-2, and 5748-6), he stated that the Nile River had changed its course and had once flowed across the Sahara, emptying into the Atlantic Ocean. This statement was verified in the 1980s when imaging radar on the space shuttle confirmed the Nile's earlier course—westward across Africa to empty into the Atlantic. On other occasions, he provided insights into the Essene community that were authenticated in the 1940s and 1950s. Given such confirmations, doesn't his story of the city in the hills and the plains demand further inquiry? Perhaps with the reopening of Iran to Western contact, the time for just such an inquiry has arrived.

Just as Homer's epics are now considered to be an important part of recorded history and the city of Troy is no longer thought to be a place of fiction, is it possible that records of Is-Shlan-doen or Toaz exist in Iran somewhere near the city of Shushtar? Was there really a city that grew from a mere stopping place for caravans to an enormous commercial, religious, and healing center that influenced an entire continent and then, somehow, was forgotten? Only time will tell.

Appendix

Edgar Cayce's eldest son, Hugh Lynn Cayce, wrote the following fictional account of the story of Uhjltd. Originally, it was intended to serve as the basis of a movie script about ancient Persia as that land was described in the Cayce readings. When the script scenario was rejected, it eventually became an A.R.E. publication that was sent to A.R.E. members who inquired about the Uhjltd period or were told that they had lived during that time.

Uhjltd
A Fictional Account of the Persian History
by Hugh Lynn Cayce

Based on readings 294-142 through 294-146

Two powerful desert tribes gathered to celebrate the marriage ceremony of two of their important families. For years these tribes had warred with each other. It was the dream of the old men that this marriage would end hostilities and bring peace. Slumdki, princess of Ra, was to become the bride of Kaila, prince of Zu.

For those who still held to the ancient teachings of their fathers who had come out of the land of the Sun, this was a great day. A priest of Egypt had been called to perform this sacred rite. His presence lent an air of mystery and reverence to the proceedings.

In silent awe the tribespeople watched their princess and prince meet and join hands before the priest. Each wore the bridal costume of their tribe. The simple garments of white were covered with symbols and figures whose meaning only the wisest remembered.

As the priest raised his hand and spoke in a foreign tongue, not a sound was to be heard except the low, tense breathing of the closely packed men and women. Suddenly his voice changed. It grew in volume and the people gasped as they began to understand the words in their own dialect:

"Hear ye! Children of the plains! Through the seed of this man and woman many people shall be blessed. Their first-born will be a son whose name shall be called Uhjltd. He will reign over you and guide you. Follow him and you will become a great people. Hear me, Prince of Zu and Princess of Ra! Thou shalt send me this son when he is twenty and one years of age. For seven years I will train him, then he will return to you. Proclaim him ruler of all your people."

For a moment the man and woman stood silent. Then Kaila spoke, "All shall be done as thou commandest, O Priest. This day before the God of our Fathers and before our peoples we pledge our first-born to the Creator in service to his fellow man."

A few years later a son was born to Kaila and Slumdki. For twenty-one years he was trained and taught according to the laws of the tribes. Peace did not come to the plainspeople and the lad Uhjltd saw his father slain in battle. But his mother remembered the vow and at the appointed time sent Uhjltd to the land of Egypt with a message to his future teacher.

Seven years passed. Again the tribes of Ra and Zu were gathered to celebrate a great event. Uhjltd was returning to become leader of his tribes. All were tense with excitement and curiosity. The older men, drawn together by their common interests, had gone aside to discuss the young man who was to rule their people.

One of the tribe of Zu first expressed the doubts and fears which were in the minds of many: "Our people have long been unhappy. Wars have not ceased. Robbers plunder our caravans, steal our camels, and carry off our young girls. This Uhjltd—will *he* be capable of meeting these troubles?

"You speak wisely," answered another of the same tribe. "We no longer prosper. We must have peace."

"That is not all we must worry over," cried one of the tribe of Ra. "Uhjltd has been away from us for a long time. He may have adopted strange customs of the foreigners. He may desert the ways of our fathers and lead our people into sin."

All turned as Remai, oldest and wisest of the tribe of Ra, began to speak: "My brothers, the blood of two great families flows in Uhjltd's veins. He will not fail us in this time of trial."

The younger men were also gathered here and there talking of their new leader, and many were the far-stretched stories they told. "Uhjltd is the mightiest of all men," one exclaimed. "Why, once when we played together I saw him withstand the full force of a great bolt of lightning from the heavens. It ran all over him but did not burn one hair of his head."

"He was the strongest of us all in running and wrestling," cried another. "There is none greater than Uhjltd."

"Perhaps this Uhjltd has changed," suggested Oujida,

one of the leaders. "Maybe he will not take advantage of our opportunity to attack the Lydians while they are so weak, busy with wars on the other side of their country. What if he is not interested in the gold, jewels and women we could capture? Suppose he will not lead us into battle, what then?" Murmurs arose here and there at this speech, but no one dared resent it openly.

Just at this point a horseman dashed up with the cry, "He is coming! Uhjltd is approaching!"

The people began to push forward and cry, "Hurrah! Long live our leader Uhjltd!" The tumult died as quickly as it began, as a lone horseman rode into view and toward the camp. A magnificent dun-colored charger pranced and turned, affected by the excitement that ran through the people and somehow aware, it seemed, of the importance of his rider.

The figure sitting so straight on the great steed was indeed one to inspire admiration. Heavy black hair fell to his shoulders. The wide forehead, the straight angular nose with its thin nostrils, the firm chin, all denoted strength of character. Steel-gray eyes were kind, even a little tear-filled, though the lips smiled. Simple, white, flowing robes failed to conceal the slender gracefulness and the corded muscles of the tanned hand and arm that held the powerful mount under control. Uhjltd, predestined leader of his people, had returned.

On either side the people called his name and his voice was clear and full as he answered. "Djhiu, how are you? How's the lance arm? And you, Ganal? Can you ride yet without falling? Ianal, how are your father and mother? Greetings! Oujida, did your last raid succeed? Well! If it isn't little Hala! What a man you've gotten to be! Ah! Father Mala! You do not change. It is good to be home again. The journey has been long, the way hard and rough."

"Son, your family waits for you in their tent. When you

have rested, all is ready for the ceremony," Remai spoke as Uhjltd dismounted and a dozen hands reached for the bridle.

Uhjltd's meeting with his two younger brothers was quiet. They were saddened by the necessity of telling him of their mother's death. He did not wait for them to speak. "Yes, I know, my brothers," he said. "She will be happy in knowing that we carry on. Do not be sad. There is much work ahead. Let us carry it together." He caught each in turn by the shoulders, shook them gently, and smiled.

A few hours later Uhjltd stood before all the assembled tribespeople. Remai spoke for the people, "Son, long ago your life was pledged to your people. Long have we waited this day. As leader of our united tribes, your responsibility is great. Robbers plunder our land, our young men fight one another, our people are unhappy.

"For seven years you have studied in the land of the Sun, the truths which were taught our fathers. You have delved into the mysteries of the gods, searched for knowledge of the laws of the Universe. You know the needs of your peoples. Into your hands we now commit the power to govern our people. May the Great One guide and protect you."

Uhjltd's answer was simple and direct, "I am ready."

Remai then placed about him the robe of the leader and Uhjltd turned to address the people. "Long have I looked forward to this day, my people. I have not forgotten the years when we fought and worked together. I have been away from you only a little while, that I might be better fitted to serve you. Long years of trial and struggle are behind us. Today we look forward to a new life. We are united. The Great One will guide us.

"Since we were little children in the tents of our fathers, we have been taught that the men and women of our tribes know no fear. Upon this great truth we shall build our nation. There is no one who would dare question the courage of our warriors, or of our women. It is a privilege to give our life's blood in support of our principles. We do not fear death.

"But there is a greater courage. Dare to uphold that which you believe to be right! Throw aside the fear that the Great One will desert you. Know that so long as you cling to the principles of loyalty, duty, courage; so long as you do not condemn your fellow man, the Great One will stand with you. My people, let us work together in harmony. My mind, my body, my life belongs to you. Stand with me and together we will approach the God of our fathers, daring to follow in the way He may direct."

During the following months Uhjltd carried out his plans for reorganization. He brought order out of chaos, peace out of strife, quiet out of tumult. The oldest and wisest men of each tribe formed a council which governed the people, made simple laws and settled differences arising between individuals and families. The camps were no longer filthy and dirty, but orderly and clean. The people now gathered each morning and evening for prayer. The services were beautiful in their simplicity and tended to develop a spirit of harmony.

With the younger men Uhjltd organized bands whose duty it was to guide and protect the caravans which passed through their country. Under this protection the commerce improved and new wealth flowed into the coffers of the merchants. Work was the keynote of the success. Men, women, and children were given something to do. The tribes began to prosper and express once more the natural joy that was part of their natures.

Two years passed. Uhjltd's younger brother, a lad of fifteen years, worshiped the leader. He followed him everywhere, continually demanding that he be allowed to help with tasks that were much too hard for him.

"Why can't I lead Diaga's band this morning?" he

asked one day. "He is sick from eating too many bananas. A caravan is due from the west, you know."

"Young man," Uhjltd answered, "I have a much more important job for you. You are to have charge today of the 'silkers' (gatherers of refuse). See that they do a good job."

"Aw, Uhjltd!" A pause, then, "Well, all right!" he answered.

That night when the lad returned tired and sore, Uhjltd met him.

"Well, Aika, I see you did a good job today!" The boy saluted in military fashion and grinned. "You can never tell," Uhjltd continued, "how many of our people you saved from the plague by your work today. Disease, you know, sometimes comes out of filth."

"Thank you," the boy answered, "but when are you going to let me do a man's work. I am as big as Rana (the older brother) already."

"The time will come soon enough," Uhjltd laughed. "Now off with you, and get ready for evening prayer."

With the growing prosperity, the people began to urge that Uhjltd select a mate, that his leadership might be continued by his children. Both the older men and the young spent many hours with him suggesting this and that alliance which would prove advantageous to the tribe. Many of the most beautiful girls in the land were brought to him that he might select a wife. In each case he refused, pointing out that his time belonged to his people, that much work was still to be done.

Finally Uhjltd's closest associates took counsel with Handra, father of Tatil—a woman famous for her beauty and noble lineage. Her father's tribe to the southwest was a powerful one and many believed that such a union would be of great advantage. Plans were laid quietly and one day Tatil came to Uhjltd's camp with her father to trade.

Though proud, having refused many offers of marriage, she was attracted to Uhjltd. Always gracious, the leader entertained the neighbors in his tent.

"Your journey was pleasant, I hope," he inquired of Handra.

"Yes, thanks to your valuable guard, we had a very pleasant journey," he answered. "I have seen the day when we could not have crossed this country without being attacked by several marauding bands."

"You honor me with your presence, Princess Tatil," Uhjltd remarked, turning toward the girl.

"The honor is ours," she answered flatteringly. "Many stories have come to us of the hospitality of the chieftain Uhjltd. They have not been exaggerated."

That night Handra and Uhjltd discussed the proposed marriage. Uhjltd's answer was the same. "You honor me, Handra, but I cannot consider marriage at this time. My people still need all my energies and time. We are at peace with your people and there is no reason why this should not continue. During the coming month our tribes gather for a great feast. Stay and honor us with your company."

Handra accepted Uhjltd's offer and set up his camp near the central camp of Uhjltd's people. For days Tatil remained in her tent, insulted and hurt over the rejection of marriage. In her desire to hurt Uhjltd she began to cultivate the friendship of his assistant and second in command, Oujida. The increasing prosperity and gradual dying down of activity among the young men offered a background for a growing unrest.

Tatil began to see Oujida daily. She spent hour after hour talking with him of his great possibilities, of his superiority to Uhjltd, of his bravery and daring. She urged him on in his plans for raids on the Lydians. Oujida began to be absent from the evening prayer. While Uhjltd noticed this, he did not approach Oujida about it, hoping that he would soon change.

Instead the condition grew worse. The young men led by Oujida began to hold secret meetings and Tatil deliberately planned a series of feasts to which she invited many of the younger men of Uhjltd's tribes. These feasts were held during the evening hour of prayer and many grew lax about attendance. Throughout this period Uhjltd held to his faith in his assistant. Many times in his meditations he prayed for Oujida.

Oujida finally excited a group of the more daring warriors to plan a raid. About a hundred gathered one evening at an appointed meeting place. "Men of Ra and Zu," Oujida cried, "have you all become cowards? Do you no longer know how to fight? To the north and west of us there is a great kingdom ripe for the picking. Great stores of gold and silver lie unguarded, ready for the taking. This very night a spy has returned bearing news of a school where Croesus's own daughter holds court, surrounded by the most beautiful women of the country.

"The king and his generals would pay well for the return of their daughters. In five days we could strike and be back in our own country. We would be heroes, and even Uhjltd would be glad to receive some of the rich booty we would bring back."

Before dawn a hundred picked men, mounted on the swiftest horses, crossed the border and rode swiftly toward the heart of the Lydian kingdom.

The guard about the school in which Elia, only daughter of King Croesus of Lydia, held her court had grown lax. The long period of peace with the nomad tribes and the growing interest in the plans to attack the Persians had drawn attention away from the southern plainsmen.

In a secluded spot away from the bustle of the growing commerce, Croesus had built a royal school. There, under the guidance of renowned teachers, the daughters of the noble families of the realm were taught the graces of the court. The scene was a beautiful one which this peaceful, unsuspecting spot presented on the night before the raid.

Most of the girls had gathered in the great hall to listen to the music of a group of wandering singers, among whom was the spy sent on ahead by Oujida to prepare the way. Surrounded by every luxury, the maidens gave themselves over to the light pleasure of the music. Silver laughter, jewels from the storehouses of the world, beauty beyond the wildest dreams of the imagination combined to furnish a background for this Elia, called "the Beautiful."

After the musicians departed, Elia—with her aunt, who was one of the instructresses; her close friend and companion Ilya, daughter of one of Croesus's ministers, and two or three of the other girls—gathered in Elia's bedchamber to read and discuss an ancient manuscript. It was the instructress who had first interested the girls in the ancient lore and legends of the first Semitic tribes. Each night they gathered to hear her read some of these almost forgotten stories. "Tonight, my dears," she began, "we will read the story of a great leader of our people who lived hundreds of years ago.

"Majara was born of a noble family, but at his birth his people were in slavery. During those days our forefathers lived far to the north of our present country. Then they did not have the great power we now have under our great king . . . " The girls settled themselves to listen to the story that was never to be finished. It was here that Oujida's men found them.

Without one false move the hawk struck in the night and the whole school was at once thrown into confusion. The gates were opened by the spy, and the guards—before they realized an enemy was upon them—died quietly at their posts. Oujida's men quickly surrounded the palace and, led by the spy, sought out the most prominent women. The daughters of the greatest families of Lydia did not succumb without a struggle. Damala, daughter of one of Croesus's noble generals, dispatched her first assailant with a dagger and died with a lance through her soft young throat. Another girl leaped from a balcony rather than be taken.

The group in Elia's bedchamber were given no opportunity to escape or harm themselves. They were bound quickly and with several others, some fifteen in all, hurried to the waiting horses.

Like the sacks of gold and jewels which had been hastily collected, the women were bound to the backs of horses brought for the purpose, then the raiders departed as quickly as they had come, leaving destruction and turmoil behind them. The pace was hard going with the added weight. And at the end of the third day Oujida realized that he would have to stop and fight the band of Lydians who had overtaken them. He realized that the pursuers would not dare attack, for fear of causing death to some of the prisoners. So he stopped, pitched camp, and sent an emissary to parley with them while he sent others on to Uhjltd to advise him of the situation. He then ordered Elia brought to his tent and sought to bargain with her to write an order for the Lydians to turn back.

"My dear princess," he began. "Our situation is most embarrassing and I find it necessary to have you write a little note for me. Here is a tablet. Kindly inform your loyal subjects that your pretty head will hang on the front of my tent before dark if they do not turn back at once."

"Dog!" she answered. "I will see your cursed hide picked by the vultures before I will aid you."

Oujida's laugh was not pleasant. He rose slowly and started toward her. "I'll see if I cannot twist a little of that spirit out of you," he said.

Elia turned to flee and fell heavily over a pile of accoutrements that lay near the door. Before Oujida could reach her the frantic girl snatched a dagger from the trappings and buried it in her breast.

Realizing that he had lost his best hostage, Oujida turned to strategy. He notified the Lydians that he would return Croesus's daughter in the morning provided they would withdraw, and proved his good faith by sending with the messenger Elia's companion Ilya and the instructress, who were only too willing to plead for her.

Fearing the anger of their king, the Lydians withdrew and waited for the coming of dawn. Oujida himself remained in camp, keeping the fires burning while he sent his men on with the loot and other prisoners. Several hours before dawn he tied Elia's dead body on a horse and drove it toward the Lydian camp, then set off quickly after his followers.

When Oujida reached the central camp where Uhjltd waited, he ordered a large part of the captured gold and the women sent to the leader. During the afternoon Uhjltd called the men of the tribes together. All wondered what attitude the leader would take and were perplexed by his silence. As soon as they were gathered, Uhjltd rose and addressed the assembly.

"Men, the peace and happiness of our people are endangered. The Lydians are now organizing an army to attack our tribes. Such a war would mean bloodshed and the destruction of all we have builded in the past few years. Now is the time for us to prove that we have a deeper kind of bravery than that which might drive us to attack our unsuspecting neighbors. Now is the time for us to dare to do what we know to be right.

"There must be no war. We must go to the Lydians with terms of peace. As your leader, I cannot ask you to do that in which I will not lead you. Here is the gold which was sent me. I will have none of it. The women I will protect in my own tents. Already I have sent messengers to notify the Lydians that both their gold and the women will be returned. At dawn I leave to carry terms of peace directly to King Croesus and beg forgiveness for the crime which he and his people have suffered at our hands."

His voice softened, and in a milder tone he continued, "Into your hands, Oujida, I commit the government of our people until I return. See that you serve them well. While I live and guide you, there will be no war. Dismiss."

When Uhjltd returned to his tents, there was great confusion and stirring. "Why can't I go with you?" Aika cried.

"No, that is impossible, lad. You must stay here to care for my household while I am away," Uhjltd answered.

"But, Uhjltd," cried the boy, "what am I to do with all these women?"

"Have I not told you before, Aika, to look for the importance in every job, every responsibility? Do you not see that by caring for and protecting the daughters of the greatest men of Lydia you will be rendering a great service?" Uhjltd reminded him gently.

"But, Uhjltd," the lad began—then stopped, smiled, and dashed off to prepare his brother's horse.

The boy spent a restless night dreaming of hundreds of women. In the morning Uhjltd departed shortly after morning prayer. The people watched him go, the old men shaking their heads sadly.

A few days later a lone plainsman approached a small oasis outside the gates of an outlying Lydian fort, and at a well beneath three palm trees sought a drink of water from a girl who sat nearby. After the Lydians had been tricked by Oujida they had come to this fort, awaiting the arrival of the army which was gathering to attack the nomad tribes.

Ilya and the instructress had come with them. The girl still mourned the fate of her companions and was bitter over Elia's death. Almost daily she sought the quiet of the oasis away from the heat and dullness of the fort. It was she who looked up at this plainsman as he approached.

"May I disturb you, maiden, for a drink from your well?" he asked, as he drew his horse up near the trees.

"It is little matter to me whether you drink or no," she answered. "It does not belong to me."

After quenching his thirst, Uhjltd looked more closely at the girl and finally decided to question her. "I have come a long way through the desert," he said. "Can you tell me if an army of Lydians have passed this way during the past few days?"

"You are quite frank about what you wish to know, aren't you?" she scoffed.

"Why should I not be?" he replied. "My people desire peace with the Lydians, and I have come to bring terms that will satisfy them."

A vague sense of uneasiness began to come over Uhjltd. Never had a meeting with a woman so affected him. Perhaps it was the indifference or the utter lack of fear, even indeed the beauty which was different from that of the usual woman of the desert.

"Are you not afraid I will call for help and have you taken?" she asked.

"Your voice would not carry to the fort," he replied lightly, "and besides, my horse is very fast."

"Ah! Such bravery," she mocked.

"Uhjltd smiled and dropped lightly down beside her. The girl laughed and rose. "I must be going," she said. "Shall I notify the commander of your arrival?"

"If you do," he answered, "I cannot meet you here at this time tomorrow."

The following day Uhjltd was waiting near the well when Ilya arrived.

"Did you inform the commander?" he asked.

"Yes," she scoffed, "but he told me that he did not have

time to chase wandering 'schanclers' (desert rats)."

"You should assure your commander that I am worthy of being chased," he answered.

"Tell me," she began earnestly, "have you heard any word of some girls who were captured from Cartha in Lydia by some desert tribes of the south? I could not rest until I had asked you."

"Had you asked me yesterday you would have saved yourself a trip," Uhjltd answered, "but I am glad you did not, for this pleasure of seeing you would have been denied me. I have seen the girls you speak of and they are safe. In fact, they were brought to me after the raid. I am the leader of the tribes you speak of. People call me Uhjltd."

"Why did you not have mercy and kill them as you did Elia?" the girl cried. "Dogs, how could you be so cruel?"

"You do not understand," Uhjltd interrupted her, "both the girls and the gold are to be returned to your people." In detail then he told her of the raid and its results, together with his plans for peace. When he had finished, the girl was silent. Revenge still burned in her heart. She saw only one face, that of Elia as she had been returned to the Lydian camp. Quickly, plans formed in her mind.

"Perhaps I can help you," she said, and Uhjltd—lost in the whirl of the totally new emotion which had suddenly come over him—failed to notice the cold gleam in her eyes and the slight twitch of the small mouth. "Tomorrow I will bring you food and water, and I will learn the plans of the army which is approaching, that you may meet them," she continued.

"If you will return again," he said, "I will be waiting for you."

The following day Ilya brought food and water and forced herself to talk with Uhjltd, drawing his attention more and more to her, so that the three men whom the commander had ordered to capture Uhjltd might approach unseen. The nomad leader suspected nothing until his horse warned him with a shrill neigh. Before he could escape the men were upon him. He surrendered without fighting.

"We shall see what other information you have for the commander," Ilya laughed cuttingly.

When brought before the leader of the fort, Uhjltd told his story simply, demanding that messengers be sent to Croesus's generals carrying his proposals. The commander was not entirely sure of just what he should do regarding Uhjltd, as many stories of his peaceful work and friendly attitude had come to him. Finally he ordered him taken to the tower and there chained hand and foot to await the return of messengers sent to the approaching army. For several days the captive was left to himself. Only bread and water were furnished him twice each day.

In the meantime the messengers sent out by the commander of the fort were captured by Oujida and a small band of his followers. On learning of Uhjltd's capture he determined to make himself the permanent leader of the tribes. The Lydian messengers were promptly run through with a lance and left dying on the desert. He sent one of his men ahead to announce Uhjltd's death and warn the people of the Lydian attack. Before the tribes could gather, however, the Lydians struck, killing many and scattering the rest in the desert. It was months before the tribe collected again, and then to wrangle over the selection of a new leader and finally break up into factions.

No news came of the death of the messengers, and Uhjltd waited in solitary confinement. He faced the situation without protest and spent much of his time in prayer and meditation. One night as he prayed for the opportunity to carry on his work, a light shone in his cell and he heard a quiet voice. "Your prayers have been heard, O Uhjltd! Prepare thyself for the valley of the shadows." After that he was even quieter, and when Ilya came to goad him into telling her more of the young girls who had been captured, he answered her softly, "I have never sought to harm your people. The words I spoke to you at the well were true."

More and more often she came to talk with him, at times bringing the instructress. Gradually they came to have faith in Uhjltd and in his plans for bringing peace to the desert. Remorse began to eat at Ilya's heart and she finally decided to aid in Uhjltd's escape. Their continued interest aroused the suspicion of the guards, and on the night before the attempt was made, as Ilya came to Uhjltd's cell to tell him of their final arrangements, she was followed by a guard who slipped to the door to listen.

"Be quiet, Uhjltd," she whispered. "Here is the key to your chains. At dawn, Irenan has arranged to have a horse at the north gate. Forgive me. Farewell."

"You are kind, Ilya," he answered. "Is there no danger for you? Come with me. I will take you safely back to your people."

"I would only hinder you," she answered. "They suspect nothing. I must go now."

When a few minutes later a cry arose in the courtyard below, Uhjltd suspected discovery. Unfastening his chains he leaped to the window and began climbing down the tower wall, just as guards with lighted torches rushed into the cell. A general alarm went up at once and a hunt for the escaped prisoner ensued. Uhjltd reached the outer wall and ran off through the shadows into the desert.

A party ordered out to search for him passed within a few yards of where he lay covered in the sand. Toward dawn Uhjltd began to whistle for his horse, which he knew had not strayed far from the fort. Just as the first rays of the sun began to light the sky, he was rewarded by the approach of the great gray. A few minutes later he set off toward his own country.

The infuriated commander of the fort ordered Ilya and Irenan brought before him. "You have betrayed your people," he cried. "While I cannot condemn you to death under our laws, there is nothing to prevent me from driving you into the desert afoot. You will be supplied with two days' rations and water. You leave at once."

Ilya's threats and pleas were no avail, and as the sun reached high noon the two were brutally cast from the walls with only a scanty supply of food and water. In the fall Irenan's leg was severely injured and Ilya was forced to almost carry her. Nothing but death awaited them.

At the end of the first day Uhjltd began to tire. Without food and water, and weakened by his long confinement, he lay down to rest on the sands. Again and again his prayers went up to the Great One to strengthen him for the work to be done. That night he dreamed of the two women who had helped him, and in his dream saw them suffering on the desert. With the coming of day he was torn between his desire to turn back and the knowledge that, weakened as he was, it would probably mean certain death. Finally he turned back toward the fort.

Toward evening he met them, barely dragging themselves along through the sands. With Irenan on the horse, and he and Ilya walking, the three set off into the desert, beginning a terrible struggle against the elements. The heat, the sand, burned and scorched them until only three living skeletons struggled on, driven by the indomitable will of the man who stopped often to pray and looked always toward the distant blur which marked the low foothills in the distance. During the afternoon of the following day the horse collapsed, falling under the weight of the two women.

"Uhjltd, save yourself," Ilya whispered feebly. "We cannot go on." She pointed to the teacher, "Irenan has no strength. I will stay with her. Go on without us."

"It is only a little farther, Ilya," he answered. "I will carry Irenan. Come, we *must* go on! The Great One will hear our pleas and answer them!"

After three long, weary days the three reached the foothills. Uhjltd placed the women in a small cave where they would be protected from the heat of the sun, and then set out to find food and water. After struggling through an increasingly rocky country for several hours, he took heart as he discovered two eagles circling about their nest some distance up on a cliff wall.

Slowly, inch by inch, he worked his way upward and then, when almost successful, slipped and fell some thirty feet to a ledge below. With the impact on the rocks there was a sickening crash as the bones in his left arm broke. Uhjltd fainted and lay as one dead. As he gradually returned to his senses, his first thought was of the women who were starving in the cave. He struggled to rise but could not. Again his plea went up to the heavens:

"O Mighty One, hear the cry of Thy son in distress! Give me strength, O Great One, to save those of Thy children whom I have led here into the desert to perish!" It was not long after this that Uhjltd again tried to drag himself back toward the cave. At the very base of the cliff on which the eagle's nest was built, he found the dead body of a desert hare. With this he continued on his tortuous way. Many times he stopped to pray, and after each time again stumbled and finally crawled on. As Uhjltd drew near the cave, he heard a feeble but welcome cry:

"Oh Uhjltd, I was so afraid you would not return! What happened? Where have you been? Come quickly, we have found water!" cried Ilya.

"Ilya," whispered Uhjltd, "the Great One has answered our prayers! We have food and water, and we shall live! Let us offer our thanks!" There in front of the little cave they offered a prayer of thanksgiving.

"O Gracious Creator of all things, we give thanks for Thy goodness! We do praise Thee for Thy infinite care of Thy children who seek Thy face! Strengthen us as we seek to carry on Thy work in whatever way Thou wouldst have us serve Thee! Increase in us, we pray, the faith in Thy ever-present care and protection!"

Uhjltd's voice changed suddenly, as he cried, "Look, Ilya!"

Like a mirage before them was a gray array of white tents. The pure whiteness was offset by the green of palm trees and wide expanses of land under cultivation.

"It is our city of the plains," Uhjltd cried. "Here we shall teach the truths of the Great One. Ilya, my arm no longer pains me. Straighten it."

"Uhjltd, you mean . . . " she began. But he interrupted her.

"I mean, Ilya, that as I have told you many times, He does not will that any should suffer. Through Him my arm is made well."

Ilya took hold of the broken arm and straightened it. Uhjltd now turned toward the cave. On his face was the look of one inspired by the presence of God.

"Irenan! Irenan!" he called. "In the name of the Great Father, arise and walk!"

There was an answering cry, and slowly, very slowly, Irenan came from the cave walking as if in a dream. She collapsed, sobbing at Uhjltd's feet. Tears of joy ran down her face, and Ilya knelt and lifted her as Uhjltd raised his face to heaven to praise the power of the great Creator.

During the following days the three began to grow stronger. The proximity of the eagles and the hare spoke of wildlife and food. Only a short distance away covered a small oasis, at the edge of the desert, fed by a mountain stream. On the fourth day Uhjltd discovered the buried remains and stores of a lost caravan. With the supplies and implements, the three were able to improve the cave and live more comfortably.

Weeks passed, and finally a small caravan was sighted. The merchant in charge was surprised and dismayed at finding the three. His caravan had wandered off the beaten path; his stores were low, and one of the men, a servant, had developed what he believed to be the plague.

After telling Uhjltd of the Lydian attack on the nomad tribes, he camped in the desert near the oasis for the night.

Afraid that the three would wish to go with him, he ordered his men to make ready to depart during the night. Taking advantage of the opportunity, he left the sick servant, whom Uhjltd found the following morning when he came to ask the merchant for supplies. Through kindness and care the man was soon restored to health. Fresh water and food cleared up the supposed plague. Gratefully, he became Uhjltd's faithful slave and soon was able to set off to the caravan route to seek help and supplies.

Days passed, and the servant finally returned with supplies and some friends, who brought one to be healed by Uhjltd. The simple faith moved Uhjltd to help the man when he was brought before him. "O Father, may Thy Spirit heal this Thy child who seeks Thy aid through me!" The man fell in a faint at Uhjltd's feet. When he was revived, he was well.

News of this incident spread, and many caravans began to pass near the oasis and the cave. Some came only to watch that which was being carried on. Others remained to study and work under Uhjltd's guidance. Most of the people who came to stay were outcasts, poor and sick, discouraged in body and mind. Uhjltd put them all to work.

The mountain stream was turned into the desert and used to irrigate land which was cultivated. Orderly rows of tents were set up, and the little colony began to take on the aspect of a busy little city. Morning and evening prayers were held, and Uhjltd propounded simple truths by which the people guided their activities.

All was peaceful and quiet. Caravan after caravan passed that way, bringing an ever-increasing stream of men and women seeking happiness. The city in the plains grew and prospered, and tales of the wonderful things that transpired there were carried throughout the adjoining countries.

One day, just as the people gathered for evening prayer, a caravan larger and richer than those which usually passed that way approached, and the leader came forward to the oasis. Uhjltd was speaking to the people, and the merchant stopped to listen on the outskirts of the crowd. The clear voice carried well in the quiet of the evening. On every face was an expression of reverence and silent awe.

"Children of the Most High, look about you upon the work of Thy Father. Has He not satisfied thy every need? Not only given you the necessities of life and substance for the physical body, but peace in mind and soul? It is not the will of the Creator that any of His children should suffer. We suffer only when we seek our own selfish desires and fail to listen to the guidance of the inner voice, which you have learned to hear.

"You came out of a world of misery and suffering, a world in which people fight for gold and power. You did not dare to do right. You were afraid, cursed by the greatest of one's enemies, the fear inwardly to stand for that which one innately feels is good. Here you are not afraid.

You dare to do that which is right. You have no fear of death through disease, starvation, and other sufferings of the physical. Here you have come to know that you *can* build within yourself that understanding of the indwelling of the Great Creative Force which will supply all needs and bring a peace beyond any understanding of the physical mind.

"The awakening of that force within can bring healing in body and mind. It has brought that to you. As you first came to begin to study these laws, you wondered at the need of constant meditation and prayer. Know ye not that it is your will which must be directed to this awakening? Long have the desires of the flesh called to you. Your mind has been turned so long toward the material life that you *will* so to live.

"Through constant meditation upon that which is pure and holy, you can awaken the divine spark and come to know yourself as a son and a daughter of the Most High. It is your privilege, your right, to seek the peace and true happiness which this closeness with the Creator brings to your mind and soul. Work! Serve your fellow humans; for in kindness, in humbleness, in purity of thought and deed, you may build an understanding of the Force which ever seeks to lift you from your own destruction. Let us work together, cooperating one with another in striving toward the goal, the full realization of the Creator within."

The man on the outskirts of the crowd was deeply impressed. He turned rather reluctantly to go, but as he moved off a hand fell on his shoulder. "Can we help you?" Uhjltd asked.

"I only stopped to ask the way to Jular," the man answered abstractedly. Uhjltd pointed to the north and east without speaking. The man continued, "You seem to have a spell over these poor devils. Some of the fantastic stories I have been hearing seem a little more real. What can you do," he added lightly, "for a sinner who is weighted down with gold?"

"Perhaps you are growing weary of your burden. Put it aside and come live here with us, where you will not need it," Uhjltd answered.

"There is no rest for me," the man replied. "I must go on."

"It is not rest, but work that I call you to do." Uhjltd's voice was compelling. "Your riches did not prevent the death of your family. Nor have they given you peace since that time. There is happiness and real rest for you in serving and teaching others. I will wait here. Go! Tell your men to depart."

As Uhjltd spoke, the man's face changed and he cried, "How did you know? All right!" He turned quickly and strode off toward his caravan. Uhjltd waited there in the shade of the palm trees. In a few minutes the caravan moved on, leaving a solitary figure standing looking after it. Edssi had come to aid Uhjltd in his work.

The new lieutenant made himself most valuable. His keen mind, trained in the markets of the world, dreamed of a great exploitation of this work. He saw the possibilities of making this city in the plains a center of ever-growing importance through its service to humankind. Many were the questions that arose concerning him, but always he kept himself clear of any criticism. He took nothing for himself, lived simply, counseled often with the teacher, and spent more and more time in silent meditation. His caravan returned bringing supplies and much needed implements; not luxuries, but tools to cultivate and work the desert soil, and writing materials on which the teachings of the leader might be set down. Again his people went forth, this time carrying messages to those in high position in other countries and long manuscripts of the leader's words of wisdom.

The day came when people of many nations arrived

in the city of tents, seeking light and understanding. From Greece, India, Egypt, and even faraway China, seekers of truth came and sat at the feet of Uhjltd, and then carried with them to their distant lands the teachings of this great leader. Thousands came to be healed, and many were the wondrous cures that were performed in the camp, both by Uhjltd and his students. Life flowed through from this center, living words that warmed the hearts and souls of people, as the sun warmed their bodies.

More and more Edssi took charge of the various activities. It was he who organized the simple courts when the need arose, and the cooperative system which simplified the trade relations of the growing city. The day came when he approached Uhjltd with plans for organizing the representatives who would go out from time to time to other lands. The people were called together and Edssi spoke to them.

"Brothers and sisters," he said, "daily we are blessed as we are privileged to work and study with our teacher Uhjltd. We live happily, at peace with the world and one another. The Great One does not hide His face from us. As we have been blessed, so we should give unto those who do not have our opportunities. I have spoken with Uhjltd, and with his full cooperation I wish to present this plan.

"Let us organize a school in which all who so desire may study, that they may be able to carry the light to distant lands. We will choose our ablest men and women to be teachers. Uhjltd himself will conduct daily study groups. There will be groups studying healing, meditation, speaking, languages, history, etc., all as a background for the teachings of our leader which have come to mean so much in our hearts.

"We will then go forth to carry them to all people, that the world may learn of the happiness it is missing in failing to pause and seek its Creator. We can no longer live within ourselves. The time has come when we must go forth to teach others through our work, our words, our lives, the truths that we have learned at the feet of this man who walks with God."

Following this meeting a small group was gathered by Edssi, and with Uhjltd, the plans were laid for the beginning of the school which grew rapidly. Students and teachers of many nations came and went, bearing tidings of the work.

Edssi worked like one inspired. He was here, there, everywhere, never sparing himself, ever urging others to greater efforts.

In all his endeavors Edssi was aided by Irenan, who—having caught a vision of the possibilities in spreading the simple truths being taught—assisted in improving and developing the presentation of the teachings to the emissaries.

It was not long before, in palace and hovel, street and marketplace around the world over, there was talk of this city of the plains and the simple truths propounded there.

One day Uhjltd received a special messenger from the land of Egypt, and at once called the people together.

"My people," he began, "the time has come when I must choose a bride. Three days hence the marriage ceremony will be held. Prepare for a period of rejoicing. One comes out of the land of the Sun who predicts that the Great One has chosen this, our humble city, as the center through which a great blessing will come to the world. There is none among us who has been more patient and long-suffering than Ilya. Before you all I do now declare her to be my accepted bride."

There was great rejoicing among the people and when at the end of the second day the ancient priest arrived, they received him reverently. A great pavilion was constructed near the cave. At the appointed time Uhjltd and Ilya came forth to stand before the priest. The trappings and hangings of the pavilion were most elaborate, the costumes of the leader and his bride were very simple.

The garment worn by the priest was light green trimmed in gold and silver. Elaborate embroidery work of signs and symbols covered it, an enormous cape of snowy white, fastened at the neck, spread in all directions. The curious headdress worn by the priest was covered with small figures cut from gold and silver, clustered about one large white diamond. All the people became silent as he raised his hand and began to speak.

"Children of the desert, you are blessed of all people. You are privileged to sit at the feet of your leader Uhjltd and listen to the truths which he explains to you, and you can then work with Edssi in spreading these truths unto all people. Even in faraway Egypt I have heard stories of your work.

"You have done your work well, Edssi—and you, Irenan. Be not weary in well-doing. Carry on. The time has come when Uhjltd, your leader, must take a bride. He has chosen one who has worked long and faithfully. I now unite these two, and proclaim that you shall call this day blessed, for you are to prepare for the coming of a great world teacher. Unto this man and woman there shall be born a son whose name shall be called Zend. The Great One has heard your pleas. This work will go on, and people will be wiser and nearer their ultimate goal because of the work which you have done. The way has been opened. May His blessings rest upon you all."

(Prepared and distributed August 1935 by the Association for Research and Enlightenment, Inc., Virginia Beach, Virginia.)

A.R.E. PRESS

The A.R.E. Press publishes quality books, videos, and audiotapes meant to improve the quality of our readers' lives—personally, professionally, and spiritually. We hope our products support your endeavors to realize your career potential, to enhance your relationships, to improve your health, and to encourage you to make the changes necessary to live a loving, joyful, and fulfilling life.

For more information or to receive a free catalog, call:

1-800-723-1112

Or write:

A.R.E. Press
215 67th Street
Virginia Beach, VA 23451-2061

DISCOVER HOW THE EDGAR CAYCE MATERIAL CAN HELP YOU!

The Association for Research and Enlightenment, Inc. (A.R.E.®), was founded in 1931 by Edgar Cayce. Its international headquarters are in Virginia Beach, Virginia, where thousands of visitors come year round. Many more are helped and inspired by A.R.E.'s local activities in their own hometowns or by contact via mail (and now the Internet!) with A.R.E. headquarters.

People from all walks of life, all around the world, have discovered meaningful and life-transforming insights in the A.R.E. programs and materials, which focus on such areas as holistic health, dreams, family life, finding your best vocation, reincarnation, ESP, meditation, personal spirituality, and soul growth in small-group settings. Call us today on our toll-free number:

1-800-333-4499

or

Explore our electronic visitors center on the
Internet: **http://www.edgarcayce.org.**

We'll be happy to tell you more about how the work of the A.R.E. can help you!

A.R.E.
215 67th Street
Virginia Beach, VA 23451-2061